Spatial Design - Breaking the 2D Paradigm

A beginner's guide to spatial design, drawing on insights from 38 industry leaders to uncover lasting ten principles and patterns in spatial design.

Foreword: Inga Petryaevskaya

Author: Dominique (Kuan-Yi) Wu

Editor: Jeremy Kress

Illustrator: Lily Pham

ISBN: 9798865974444

Cover design by: Dominique (Kuan-Yi), Wu
Printed in the United States of America

This book is dedicated to Jeremy, Sadie, Giggy, Marc, Lily, along with the dedicated staff at XReality Pro, Kate and Homan.

Special thanks to my mom, my sister Cindy, and my family in Taiwan.

This is for everyone who has supported me, those aspiring to join the spatial design industry, and all the XR & Spatial Computing Leaders guiding us toward the future.

"I'm with Jaron Lanier, who likes to describe the most amazing moment in VR as the moment when you take the HMD off and are flooded with the full gamut of subtle sensory inputs that VR can't capture—fine gradations of light, smells, the sensation of air moving on your skin, the weight and torque of the headset in your hand—these are all sensations that are incredibly difficult, if not impossible, to effectively simulate in a virtual world." — Jeremy Bailenson, Experience on Demand: What Virtual Reality Is, How It Works, and What It Can Do

Contents

Foreword

It's hard to imagine a better time for this book to come into our hands. We're at a turning point where the platform shift to spatial computing has finally become a reality. The hardware we need is not just powerful, but also comfortable to use, affordable, and ready for everyone. This is the perfect moment to start creating content that fully uses the power and potential of immersive media and blended realities.

There's a growing need for spatial applications, and users are looking for more exciting and engaging experiences. The bar and expectations for the user experience have grown as well. This book is like a guiding light, full of useful tips and clear strategies that are important for designing apps in this exciting but very new immersive medium. While reading, I often thought about how much this book would have helped me back in 2017 when I first started making apps for head-mounted displays. It would have been incredibly valuable, saving us a lot of time and effort in figuring out what works best to keep users highly engaged and minimize friction while they learn new types of inputs and interactions, especially when using a completely new kind of hardware device worn right on their face. It's an ongoing search for answers. We're always asking why users should wear this device and how to make experiences that clearly make sense to them. Invent new types of interactions, but at the same time, stay familiar and accessible to minimize the overall friction. While designing spatial apps we keep looking for those amazing, magical moments that bring out new emotions through new kinds of interactions.

In spatial apps, user experience (UX) is not just a component; it's the cornerstone. It's the key to getting people excited about using the app, keeping them engaged, and bringing them back. Dominique Wu, an experienced XR designer, delves deep into the nuances of UI and UX for spatial applications. Whether it's crafting a fully immersive VR journey, a Mixed Reality experience, or applications for AR glasses, Dominique guides you through the labyrinth of design challenges specific to spatial apps, dismantling traditional flat screen paradigms with every step.

This book is perfect for any 2D or 3D UI/UX or interaction designer who's excited about the future of spatial computing and wants to get into XR design. It's also great for experienced XR designers, offering a wealth of knowledge, examples, and analyses of successful apps and UI/UX findings. Dominique has talked to many top experts and influencers in XR, and she always connects theory with practical, real apps and game examples. I also find it a very useful read for product owners and producers of XR experiences to set their expectations high and speak the same language with the design team.

More than a technology book, it's a journey into the heart of UI/UX design for extended reality, engaging and accessible in its narrative. I envision designers eagerly reading through these pages, then donning their headsets to immediately explore and experiment with the concepts and applications they've just discovered.

In this era of spatial computing, this book doesn't just inform; it inspires and empowers, offering a window into an augmented world where design transcends screens and enters the realm of immersive, interactive experiences.

Inga Petryaevskaya

Founder, CEO, ShapesXR

Acknowledgments

This book is a culmination of insights, support, and guidance from numerous individuals to whom I owe immense gratitude.

Firstly, I extend my deepest appreciation to my family—my mother, my younger sister, and my partner, Jeremy Kress.

Jeremy, your dedication in assisting with the editing, especially during those midnight hours, and your meticulous attention to detail in categorizing and naming each pattern, building block, illustration, and principle have been invaluable. Your expertise as a professional editor and a software/hardware engineer has greatly enriched this work.

To our beloved pets, Sadie, and Giggy, thank you for being constant companions throughout this journey.

I am grateful to the XReality Pro team, especially Marc Mathys for your advice and mentorship. A special mention to Lily Pham, Kateryna Bielotserkovska, and Homan Chou for your unwavering support and contributions to all our XReality projects. Lily, your ability to learn anything swiftly and deliver professionally is truly remarkable.

To Inga Petryaevskaya, thank you for writing the Foreword and for your kind words. Your achievements with ShapesXR, a pioneering XR prototype tool, are inspiring. Your support for me and XReality Pro is greatly appreciated.

The insights shared by 38 XR industry leaders interviewed for this book have been pivotal. Each of you has contributed uniquely to the XR industry, and I extend my heartfelt thanks to Ori Inbar, Charlie Fink, Amy LaMeyer, Julie Smithson, Alan Smithson, Lorelle VanFossen, David Colleen, Ben Erwin, Terry xR. Schussler, Susan Cummings, and Robin Moulder for your invaluable time and wisdom.

To my UX peers, including Ruth Diaz, John Hanacek, Deirdre V. Lyons, Alex Fernandez, and Paul Hoover, thank you for multiple insightful interviews that helped me grasp the current trends and wisdom in the UX and XR fields.

I also want to acknowledge the women leaders in the XR industry for their enlightening insights. Karen Stritzinger, Gigi Johnson, Cecilia Uhr, Rahel Demant, and Estella Tse, your perspectives have added invaluable diversity to this book.

Lastly, I am indebted to all the XR industry leaders who are at the forefront in various fields such as medical, development, accessibility, AI, gaming, data, press, metaverse building, architecture, and education. My gratitude goes to Kyle Morrand, Amir Bozorgzadeh, Chris McNally, Sam Hessenauer, Thomas Van Bouwel, Lee Vermeulen, Antony Vitillo, Damon Hernandez, Ferhan Özkan, Jim Conrad, Jason Marsh, Dirk Schmidt, Jason Shuster, Chris Castaldi, and Frank Shi for your time and expertise.

This book strives to diversify the conversation in XR and spatial computing fields which were historically shaped by the contributions of highly skilled men. My narrative includes founding startups and serving as a UX designer at prominent companies such as Meta and Walmart, with a focus on XR and spatial computing projects. As an Asian woman under 40, my journey to U.S. citizenship spanned a decade, beginning with a working visa in 2011 and getting citizenship in 2022. This diverse background has enriched my experience in the technology and experience design industry. This book aims to cultivate a wider array of voices within these sectors. It serves as a rallying call for women, people from diverse backgrounds and ethnicities, and the younger generation, motivating them to actively participate and contribute to the dynamic and rapidly evolving landscape of these cutting-edge technologies.

Finally, thanks to all the interviewees who participate in the book creation (A-Z):

Alan Smithson - Co-Founder of METAVRSE
Alex Fernandez - Co-Founder of Nspire

Amir Bozorgzadeh - CEO of Virtuleap

Amy LaMeyer - Managing Partner at the WXR Fund

Antony Vitillo - CTO at VRROOM

Ben Erwin - Creator of The Poly Awards

Cecilia Uhr - Co-Founder of Bezi

Charlie Fink - Columnist at Forbes

Chayan Vinayak - Founder of Takdhin-Tv

Chris Castaldi - Technical Director at 3lbXR

Chris McNally - Co-Founder of iMcNally

Damon Hernandez - CEO of Mixx Reality

David Colleen - CEO of SapientX

Deirdre V. Lyons - Co-Founder of Ferryman Collective

Dirk Schmidt - CEO of BizzTech

Estella Tse - XR Creative Director & Artist

Ferhan Özkan - Co-Founder of XR Bootcamp

Frank Shi - Co-Founder of Paper Triangles

Gigi Johnson - President at Rethink Next

Inga Petryaevskaya - CEO of ShapesXR

Jason Marsh - CEO of Flow Immersive

Jason Shuster - COO at BizzTech

Jim Conrad - Senior Designer at Mozilla

John Hanacek - XR Interaction Designer at Nanome Inc

Julie Smithson - Co-Founder of METAVRSE

Karen Stritzinger - Founder of Old Hara Studios

Kyle Morrand - CEO of 302 Interactive

Lee Vermeulen - Founder of Alientrap

Lorelle VanFossen - Director of Educators in VR

Ori Inbar - Founder of Super Ventures and AWE

Paul Hoover - Head of Design at ShapesXR

Rahel Demant - Co-Founder of XR Bootcamp

Robin Moulder - CEO of 3lbXR

Ruth Diaz - Co-founder and CVO of inPath XR

Sam Hessenauer - Co-Founder & CTO of Nanome Inc

Susan Cummings - CEO/Co-Founder of Tiny Rebel Games (creators of Petaverse)

Terry xR. Schussler - Sr. Director of XR & Spatial Computing at Deutsche Telekom

Thomas Van Bouwel - VR Developer at Cubism & Laser Dance

Introduction

This book leads creators beyond 2D design, drawing on insights from 38 industry leaders to uncover lasting principles and patterns in spatial design. Aimed at creators eager to venture into XR and spatial computing design, this book emphasizes the shift from traditional 2D design principles—centered around GUI elements like menus and buttons—to a more holistic, human-centered approach in spatial design. It transcends mere visual components, integrating aspects of psychology, physicality, technology, safety, and policy. The focus is not just on comfortable interactions on 2D screens but on crafting safe, satisfying digital worlds where humans can coexist with technology. Covering Augmented Reality (AR), Virtual Reality (VR), Mixed Reality (MR), Extended Reality (XR), and Spatial Computing, this book is not meant as an exhaustive tech resource, but as a primer on core concepts. It empowers readers to apply these design patterns in their future projects.

My engagement in VR and AR, starting in 2017 and including work at companies like Meta and Walmart (Store 8), evolved into a formal pursuit in 2021, where I began establishing spatial design guidelines that extended beyond gaming. This led to my participation in the 2022 Augmented World Expo (AWE), highlighting the lack of standard UX principles in this field. In response, I interviewed 38 XR and spatial design leaders, blending their insights with strategic and technical viewpoints to navigate the evolving spatial design landscape. This book marks the start of a journey to unearth timeless patterns in spatial design. As the field progresses, characterized by devices merging immersive Virtual Reality with augmented real-world experiences, this guide prepares readers for the future of UX design. It encourages moving beyond the 2D paradigm, advocating for immersive experiences crafted with new UX design principles for three-dimensional spaces. Amy LaMeyer, Managing Partner at the WXR Fund, emphasizes the *3Cs* (Comfort, Cost, and Content) for broader XR adoption from the headset adoption aspects. Cost, Comfort, and Content. Cost addresses not only the affordability of XR technologies but also their durability and long-term value. Comfort is about the user experience, ensuring both the physical ease of using XR devices and their user-friendliness. Finally, the content is about problem-solving capabilities and life-simplifying aspects to its potential for providing engaging and entertaining experiences, underlining that XR's success hinges on the quality and relevance of its content. This book is about the comfort aspect for broader XR adoption echoing Amy said.

Spatial computing, blending the virtual and physical worlds, is a central theme, promoting an immersive, 3D interaction with both. The book explores the transition from a predominantly 2D digital world to a three-dimensional spatial computing era, highlighting the resulting opportunities and challenges. Readers will learn about the convergence of spatial, experience, and AI design; how to craft immersive designs; the ten principles of spatial design; patterns and building blocks; and insights into future trends and preparations for them.

1

Convergence of Spatial, Experience and AI

"XR is the interface of AI."
-Ori Inbar

In the article *Why Spatial Computing is the Future of Work and Play*[1] Brian Wallace mentioned that in the future, spatial computing will be applied in work, play, education, and Health. Envision a world where our environment becomes an extension of our minds, equipped with the sensory depth of human perception. Marrying environmental consciousness with AI and visual simulations, objects could perceive our desires, offering guidance and suggestions with precision. This seamless integration promises a new era of interaction, where our physical spaces become intelligent companions in our quests. The technologies encompass robotics, vehicles, GPS, GIS, IoT, Digital Twins, AI, XR spatial visualization, and more.

History: From XR Evolution to Spatial Artificial Intelligence

In the expanding realm of spatial design, visionaries like David Colleen, CEO of SapientX, foresee objects with AI transforming into sentient entities. David also points out the current phase of Extended Reality (XR) evolution, identifying it as the fourth wave. Through history, we can see that XR is merging with spatial computing and AI enhancement. David outlines the progression of XR technology in four waves:

1. The first wave (pre-internet) began in 1960 and it was characterized by walkthrough VR experiences, where the equipment used was bulky, expensive, and experimental.

---

[1] Anewdomain.net, https://anewdomain.net/why-spatial-computing-is-the-future-of-work-and-play, accessed Jan. 2024.

2. The second wave emerged in 1995 with VRML (virtual reality modeling language), marked by the ability to share 3D experiences and VR content online via web browsers, allowing anyone to publish VR content. This enabled the first 3D, multi-user metaverses. In 2002, Karen Marcello brought this web-based 3D together with the Alicebot conversational AI system to create the first 3D, AI talking character for an Australian performance artist named Stelarc. The following year, Karen joined Planet 9 Studios where she helped to develop the Sage talking character platform which used Act-R as an AI reasoning system.

Fig. 1.1: Sage

3. The third wave started in 2014 and it was defined by the introduction of low-cost Head-Mounted Displays (HMDs), like the Oculus Rift, which made VR more immersive and it introduced a new audience to augmented reality. In 2022. SapientX brought AI powered talking characters into AR initially using the Unity game engine and the Xreal glasses and later added support for Apple ARkit.

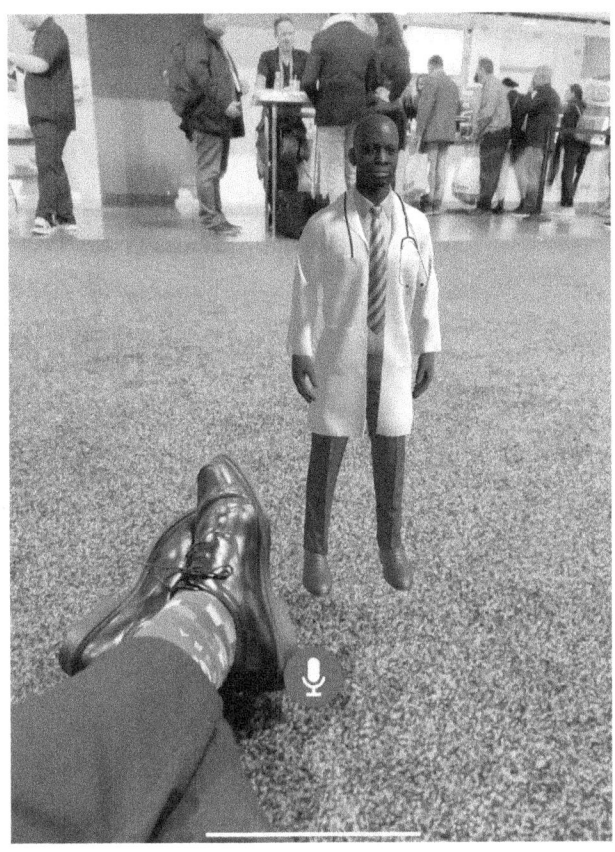

Fig. 1.2: Hank, a conversational health clinic character running in ARkit on an iPad.

4. The present fourth wave of XR marks a substantial shift towards mixed reality experiences. In this phase, the experience of XR is greatly simplified, with users needing only to wear a pair of glasses. This signifies a trend towards more seamless and integrated mixed reality experiences. David highlighted that the use of advanced AR glasses like those from Bose, XREAL, and Ray-Ban represents a new era in XR. These glasses facilitate interaction through voice commands, and in the future, they are expected to offer visual displays and interactive capabilities, further enhancing the way XR assists people in their daily activities.

As technology progresses, we witness machines emulating human traits—seeing, learning, and even smelling—pushing boundaries of what's possible. In the era of spatial computing and AI, the blending of virtual and real worlds will be profound. Physical objects will gain the capability to interact with humans through Natural User

Interfaces (NUI) like eye movements, hand gestures, and voice commands. These objects will be equipped with AI 'brains' for advanced data processing, 'eyes' for visual recognition, and 'mouths' for speech communication. This integration will create a seamless interaction between humans and their environment, revolutionizing how we interact with technology.

AR, VR, XR, and Spatial Computing. Which One is Which?

Terry Schussler, senior director of XR & Spatial Computing at Deutsche Telekom, aptly stated, "We can easily get lost in terminology." Terry recalled how in the 1990s, there was much debate over how to define the dot-com boom. Now, there's no need to explain what the "internet" is; the term is universally understood. Similarly, with AR, VR, MR, XR, and spatial computing, the specific nomenclature is less important than how users engage with the technology. He pointed out that Snapchat didn't set out to define AR; instead, it empowered creators to make AR lenses and users to interact with them. Over time, as usage grew, the public began to recognize those filters as AR lenses. Terry believes understanding of AR—and by extension, XR and spatial computing—will come from practical use, not from the terms themselves. It's the hands-on experience that will eventually demystify these technologies for the masses. Here is what we currently understand about its uses. However, as we learn to create and utilize these technologies, we will become familiar with them and won't need explanations. You may be unfamiliar with the terms AR, VR, MR, XR, Spatial Computing, and AI, so a brief description is provided below.

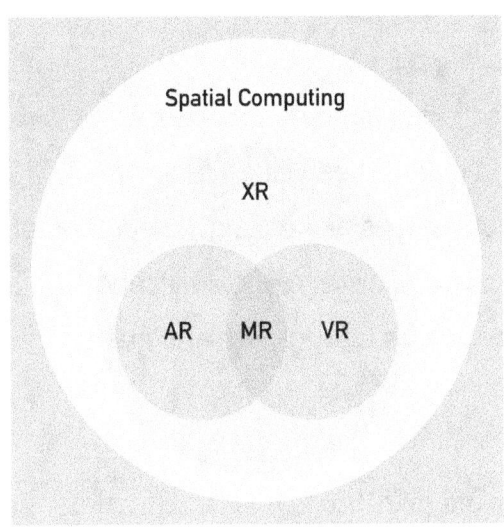

Fig. 1.3: Spatial computing is an umbrella term encompassing Virtual, Augmented, and Mixed Reality (collectively known as "Extended Reality" or XR), as well as physical systems such as robotics and autonomous vehicles.

Extended Reality (XR)

Extended Reality (XR) is a collective term for immersive technologies, which include Augmented Reality (AR), Virtual Reality (VR), and Mixed Reality (MR). Spatial computing, a broader category encompassing XR, involves understanding the physical world and using computational power to create interactive virtual representations within it. The ongoing trend in the industry suggests that XR is gradually merging with spatial computing, as seen in the evolving technologies of Mixed-Reality devices like the Quest 3 and upcoming Meta devices. These developments are indicative of a shift from purely XR-focused technology to a more comprehensive spatial computing approach that incorporates a wider array of technologies.

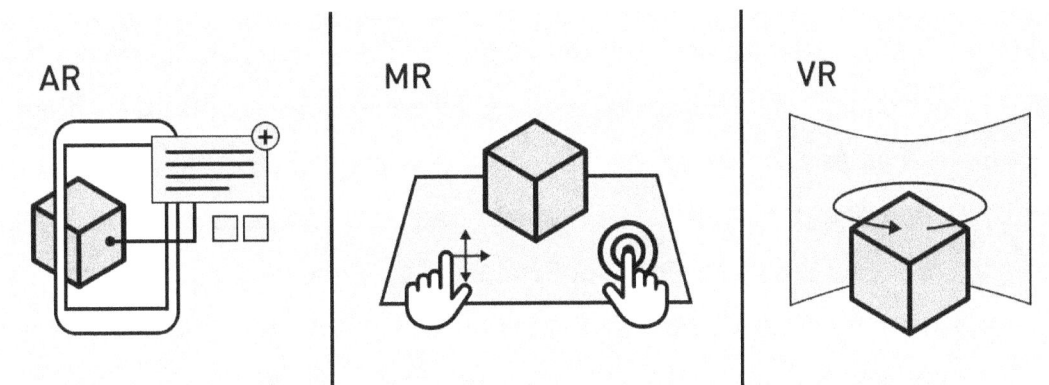

Fig. 1.4: Augmented Reality (AR) overlays digital information onto real-world views, Mixed Reality (MR) blends real and virtual worlds for interactive experiences, and Virtual Reality (VR) creates fully immersive digital environments. XR encompasses all these technologies, forming a spectrum from real to virtual environments.

Spatial Computing

The integration of advanced technologies is poised to significantly enhance the convenience of our lives. Higher engagement with daily activities will be facilitated by more intuitive interfaces, which will increasingly become 'invisible' through natural inputs like eye movement, hand gestures, and voice commands. This evolution will lead to smarter environments where everything can interact with us through advancements in AI and deep learning.

Spatial computing, initially defined by Simon Greenwold in 2003, is characterized as "*human interaction with a machine where the machine maintains and manipulates references to real objects and spaces.*"[2] More recently, this concept was further advanced when Apple introduced a spatial computing platform featuring the Vision Pro on June 5, 2023.

Spatial computing transcends 2D data and logic integration, merging them with 3D-contextualized information to blend physical and digital realities more effectively. It leverages sensors, photogrammetry, IoT, VR, AR, GPS, robotics, vehicle, digital twins, and AI to recognize and map environments, offering immersive and digitally enhanced real-world interactions. The technologies of spatial computing include navigation enhancement such as GPS using real-time data overlays to guide the user through their physical environment, computer vision systems that can recognize and respond to what cameras and sensors are observing; depth sensing used for creating accurate 3D representations of physical spaces; eye tracking used for recognizing individuals as well as their conscious and unconscious responses to external stimuli; gesture recognition used primarily to control spatial design environments without the need for physical controllers; haptic feedback providing the sense of touch and physical presence in digital environments; AI which allows for intelligent and simple interaction between human, environment and digital systems.

---

[2] Greenwold, Simon (June 2003). "Spatial Computing". MIT Graduate Thesis. Retrieved 22 December 2019.

Artificial Intelligence (AI)

Artificial Intelligence (AI) is a branch of computer science focused on creating machines or software that exhibit intelligence, distinguishing it from natural human or animal intelligence. Its applications are vast, including advanced web search engines, recommendation systems, understanding human speech, self-driving cars, creative tools like ChatGPT, and superhuman capabilities in strategy games. The goal of general intelligence (AGI), where machines can handle any intellectual task that a human being can. A level of artificial intelligence where a machine can understand, learn, and apply its intelligence broadly and flexibly, like a human's cognitive abilities.

Spatial Artificial Intelligence

Ori Inbar, the Founder of Super Ventures, and AWE, underscored the growing convergence of XR and AI. He envisioned a future where XR and AI are seamlessly integrated, to the point where they might be indistinguishable, and proposed the term SPAI (Spatial Artificial Intelligence) to reflect this fusion. He envisions AR being used extensively in daily life, allowing users to see the real world with additional content superimposed in a way that is indistinguishable from reality.

Ori credited the advancements in AR and VR to breakthroughs in machine learning and AI. Spatial AI, or Geospatial AI, is an evolving field that combines AI with spatial data analysis, enabling machines to understand and analyze spatial relationships and patterns in data. By integrating various geospatial data sources, such as satellite imagery, GPS data, and geographic information systems (GIS), with AI algorithms, Spatial AI empowers machines with the ability to derive insights, predict outcomes, and execute complex tasks in the physical world. This technology is crucial in multiple domains, including autonomous vehicle navigation, urban planning for infrastructure, and agriculture for crop monitoring and yield assessment. Leveraging tools like computer vision and AI, Spatial AI marks a significant leap in how machines comprehend and interact with spatial settings.

Further, Ori discussed AI's role in enhancing natural interactions within XR technology. He acknowledged the current limitations of XR, noting its significant growth yet lack mainstream adoption. Ori emphasized the need for the coming decade to focus on integrating XR and spatial design into everyday life, akin to the ubiquity of smartphones. He recognized the challenges in this ambition, particularly in advancing hardware, cautioning that progress might be slower than expected due to the complexities of physics and optics. Here are some features of Spatial Artificial Intelligence (SPAI):

1. **Sensors and Cameras:** Devices use a combination of sensors and cameras to scan and interpret the physical environment. These can include depth sensors, motion trackers, and RGB cameras.

2. **Environmental Mapping:** Through these sensors, the device creates a digital map of the surrounding area. This process, often called SLAM (Simultaneous Localization and Mapping), allows the device to understand the layout and dimensions of the space, identifying walls, floors, objects, and even people.

3. **Object Recognition:** Advanced spatial design systems can recognize and differentiate between various objects and features within the environment. This can be achieved through machine learning algorithms that have been trained to identify specific shapes, textures, or patterns.

4. **Spatial Awareness:** The device continuously updates its understanding of its position and orientation in relation to the environment. This is crucial for accurately overlaying digital content onto the real world.

5. **Data Processing and Rendering:** All the data collected by the sensors is processed in real time to render digital content that interacts seamlessly with the real world. This requires significant computational power and sophisticated software algorithms.

Apple, Meta, Samsung, Qualcomm, Google, Varjo, and Lynx currently lead the market for mixed reality technology. Through the high quality of hardware and innovative mixed reality creators and games, companies such as Boeing and Lowe's will help accelerate mixed reality technology.

Boeing, collaborating with augmented-reality specialist Red 6, has successfully tried a cutting-edge virtual display system aboard a TA-4J Skyhawk tactical aircraft. This significant step paves the way for the system's future integration into the T-7 advanced training jet. The system allows pilots to engage with virtual aircraft and threats, both on the ground and airborne, during actual flights. This provides a highly realistic training environment while significantly reducing physical risks.

In a related development, Lowe's has upgraded its app by incorporating augmented reality. It has added the Craftsman collection and more than 500 other products, enabling customers to visualize these items in their personal spaces prior to purchase. The "View in Your Space" feature, designed for Android ARCore devices, empowers users to place and evaluate life-like, proportionally accurate products in actual environments. This enhances the decision-making process and overall shopping experience.

Spatial Design

The Convergence of XR and Spatial Artificial Intelligence

The two leading headsets for spatial computing and mixed reality are Vision Pro and Quest 3. On June 5, 2023, Apple unveiled the Vision Pro at its Worldwide Developers Conference, branding it as a "Spatial Computing Device." This move appeared to signal Apple's intention to move beyond the conventional AR/VR/XR terminology, pivoting towards the concept of spatial computing. Consequently, XR design began to evolve into spatial design, a shift propelled by Apple's entry into the spatial device arena. This raises pertinent questions: What are the distinctions and parallels between XR and spatial computing devices?

Apple's Vision Pro, representative of spatial computing, though initially distinct in its design philosophies and intended use cases, has started to exhibit significant overlaps in functionality and purpose. This convergence reflects the evolving landscape in immersive technology, where the lines between different terminologies and technologies are increasingly blurring, leading to a unified approach in designing and developing devices that are versatile in their application and immersive in their experience. Apple, while positioning itself in the spatial computing category, does not use a see-through (transparent glasses) approach. Instead, it adopts a method more akin to XR devices to fulfill its spatial computing aspirations. The Vision Pro also transitions from traditional graphical user interfaces (GUI) to natural user interfaces (NUI) by eliminating controllers. Conversely, Quest 3 is evolving its controller system to embrace eye-hand coordination, shifting its focus from purely VR to a more mixed-reality approach, encompassing room understanding and environmental interaction.

The Quest 3 transitions into mixed reality (MR), adding features like room scanning, understanding spatial layouts, and depth perception in the environment. This marks the beginning of what is known as spatial computing - the ability to comprehend and interact with one's surroundings. Thus, strictly speaking, the Quest 3 can also be considered a spatial computing device due to its ability to overlay and interact with the environment, a key feature of mixed reality. On the other hand, the Apple Vision Pro, despite its claim as a "spatial computing" device, is still in its early stages, being the inaugural product in Apple's spatial computing line.

The Quest 3 targets gaming and consumer markets, as well as enterprise applications, while the Vision Pro is aimed primarily at the enterprise sector but also caters to consumers, transforming 2D app experiences into 3D. Despite differing terminology, both devices are quite similar in capability, though the Apple Vision Pro, being more expensive, boasts a superior tracking system and passthrough functionality compared to the Quest 3. Given their similar capabilities and directions, a convergence with other technologies, like true spatial computing devices, seems imminent.

As Terry Schussler suggests, people may not recall the specific terminology but will remember the use cases. Therefore, in this book, to simplify terminology, we will refer to the design principles for both XR devices (like Quest 3) and Spatial devices (like Apple Vision Pro) as "Spatial Design."

Conclusion

The convergence of Spatial, Experience, and AI represents a monumental shift in how we interact with technology and perceive our environment. From Ori Inbar's vision of an indistinguishable blend of XR and AI in Spatial Artificial Intelligence (SPAI) to the pioneering steps of companies like Boeing and Lowe's in integrating augmented reality into practical applications, we are witnessing a significant transformation. The evolution of XR through its four waves, as outlined by David Colleen, reflects a journey towards more intuitive, seamless mixed-reality experiences, now being realized in devices like Quest 3 and Apple's Vision Pro.

These advancements signal a future where our interactions with technology are more natural and integrated into our daily lives, thanks to the fusion of spatial computing, immersive technologies, and AI. The distinctions between AR, VR, XR, and Spatial Computing are becoming less relevant as the focus shifts to how these technologies enhance human experience. As we embrace this era of Spatial Design, we step into a world where our physical and digital realities merge, offering unprecedented opportunities for innovation, creativity, and engagement in every aspect of our lives. This convergence not only reshapes the landscape of technology but also redefines the boundaries of human experience and interaction.

2

The Designer Revolution

"The illiterate of the 21st century will not be those who cannot read and write, but those who cannot learn, unlearn and relearn." – Alvin Toffler

Spatial AI technology marks a significant shift from traditional design roles to modern spatial design roles, evolving from 2D interfaces to dynamic 3D environments. This transition encompasses several key areas for designers and creators:

1. **Job Duty Evolution:** The shift in job responsibilities reflects a move from specialized skills to a holistic understanding of problem-solving. Designers are now expected to expand their expertise beyond basic graphic design tools to encompass a wide range of abilities, including coding, development, design, user experience, 3D environments, as well as business and policy insights.

2. **Specialist to Generalist:** The trend has shifted from having niche skills to gaining a comprehensive grasp of a broader spectrum in design. This includes AI, technology, psychology, storytelling, 3D space design, policy, business, hardware inputs, software development, and user experience.

3. **Critical Thinking:** Critical thinking remains essential, demanding the analysis of facts, evidence, observations, and arguments to reach rational, skeptical, and unbiased conclusions.

4. **Resilience:** Qualities such as resilience, an experiential approach, and robust problem-solving skills are increasingly important, complemented by a fearless attitude toward facing failure.

Job Duty Revolution

In 2000, expertise in Photoshop and Illustrator was highly valued for graduates entering the graphic design field. However, as digital needs evolved, so did the required skills. By 2011, the rise of Web Design as a separate discipline signaled an industry shift. The emergence of UX design in 2013 further changed the landscape, leading many designers to specialize in this new area. The term extended reality (XR) was introduced in 1991.[3] More recently, XR encompasses AR, VR, and MR, merging the physical and digital worlds, and offering immersive experiences. This field gained additional momentum with Mark Zuckerberg's 2021 announcement of Facebook's transformation into Meta, emphasizing the growing significance of the Metaverse concept.

This trajectory continued in 2023 with the announcement of Apple Vision Pro, which brought spatial computing to the forefront, making spatial design a key skill in 2024. This progression underscores a trend where not only are the skills required in design expanding from graphic to spatial design, but there's also a growing need for designers to understand both the business and technological aspects of their work. Here are how designers transfer from graphic design to spatial design.

Graphic: Design

Graphic design is *"a craft where professionals create visual content to communicate messages."*[4] Graphic design requires a solid understanding of essential design principles, layout strategies, color theory, and typography, along with a grasp of design history. Typical projects in this field range from designing posters and packaging to crafting branding identities. Understanding branding, business, the form of products, and the design topic with research skills is needed. It serves as a visual presentation of a business, agenda, and product. Distinct from interactive or digital design, graphic design emphasizes the importance of aesthetic form in conveying its design concept. It

---

[3] Mann, S., and Wyckoff, C., "Extended Reality", MIT 4-405, 1991

[4] Interaction Design Foundation, *What is Graphic Design?*, *https://www.interaction-design.org/literature/topics/graphic-design*, *accessed Jan. 2024*

is an artistic method aimed at enhancing product promotion and explanation, primarily through visual means rather than through direct interaction with machines or computers.

User Experience (UX): Design + Experience

UX encompasses the full spectrum of an end-user's interaction with a company, including its services and products. *UX design involves the design of the entire process of acquiring and integrating the product, including aspects of branding, design, usability, and function.*[5] This field is vital in the realms of product, web, and app development, requiring designers to be well-rounded in design theory, like graphic design, and adept in research, user testing, and grasping development processes. A UX designer's key responsibilities include making a product or service usable, enjoyable, and accessible, and integrating user feedback. This diverse role calls for a combination of essential skills in design, interaction, and business. It enables designers to understand the broader context of a product and to actively participate in the product development pipeline, seamlessly merging design expertise with interactive elements.

XR Design: UI Design + 3D + Technology

"XR design" extends beyond traditional design skills, research, communication, and interaction, necessitating proficiency in 3D design due to its incorporation of 'z' space, which is pivotal for immersive storytelling. In its nascent stages, XR tools were challenging to master compared to conventional design tools, presenting a relatively steep learning curve. Many XR designers originated from fields such as software development, 3D modeling, architecture, animation, business, film, and more. It requires extensive development and 3D skills, as well as a willingness to experiment with new technologies. Predominantly developers and engineers found XR to be an exciting arena for pioneering new technologies. However, early XR designs often prioritized technological experimentation over user comfort, leading to many XR apps and games that were impressive but caused discomfort or dizziness. This initial phase tarnished

---

[5] Interaction Design Foundation, https://www.interaction-design.org/literature/topics/ux-design, accessed Feb. 2024

VR's reputation, associating it with an uncomfortable and heavy headset experience. Despite significant improvements in devices like Meta Quest 3, there remains a hesitancy to re-engage with XR due to past negative experiences. Thus, XR design represents a fusion of user interface aesthetics, interactive dynamics, and three-dimensional creativity, focusing on both the exhibition of technological advancement and the continuous enhancement of user comfort and experience.

Spatial Design: UX + 3D + Technologies + AI

On Apple's website, during WWDC2023, a video titled "Principles of Spatial Design" was announced, which redefined the concept of Spatial Design. It redefined Spatial Design as "...to be **human-centered...**use dimension to take advantage of the space and push apps even further with **immersion**... make apps that feel **authentic** to the platform...strike a balance with what's **familiar**."[6] So in short, spatial design is: "*A human-centered, immersive experience that resonates with authenticity, ensuring interactions are familiar and seamless.*"

Spatial design, initially emerging in 2003 and applied in devices like HoloLens and Magic Leap, was primarily utilized in the business sector due to its costly production and specialized development skills, thus limiting widespread public adoption. Apple revolutionized this domain in 2024 with the launch of Vision Pro, introducing a new paradigm in spatial computing.

Unlike VR headsets that require creating a 'guardian' system to prevent physical injuries, Vision Pro allows users to see the real world directly, negating the need for such safeguards. This contrasts with VR's reliance on guardians due to the disconnect between virtual and physical spaces, often requiring extensive tutorials. Vision Pro's "no controllers" fundamentally changes the user experience design. Unlike XR's approach of overlaying buttons and providing controller tutorials, Vision Pro integrates digital

---

[6] Apple, Principles of spatial design: https://developer.apple.com/videos/play/wwdc2023/10072, accessed Jan. 2024

content with physical space using Natural User Interfaces like voice, eye, and hand gestures without controllers. This shift poses new challenges in interface navigation and promotes a more intuitive interaction with digital content, akin to real-world interactions. Apple's approach to spatial design prioritizes 'Comfort' and 'Human-Centered', an element somewhat overlooked in XR design.

Moreover, Vision Pro's design principles and privacy protocols emphasize 'Safety and Security' as a fundamental aspect of spatial design. The shift from XR to spatial computing marks a significant and permanent transformation. In this convergence of physical and digital realms, human-machine interactions integrate smoothly. Apple has been instrumental in reshaping this new era of spatial computing, with a strong emphasis on experience-centric design. The emergence of AI and user-friendly no-code tools simplifies content creation, making it as easy as using drag-and-drop or responding to voice or text commands. AI plays an indispensable role in this progression, managing complex operations and expediting the growth of spatial computing and design.

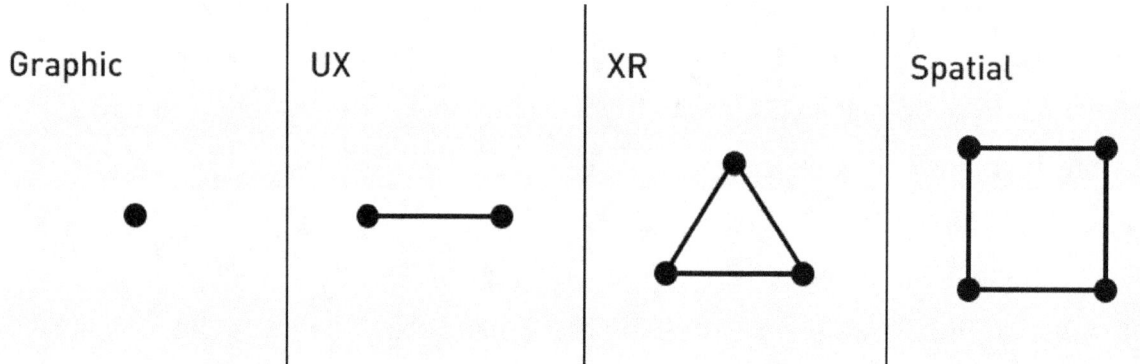

Fig. 2.1: The graphic design centers on aesthetics, UX design bridges aesthetics with user experience, XR design integrates aesthetics, 3D elements, and technology, while Spatial Design unifies design, 3D, technologies, and AI.

Specialist to Generalist

Most XR and spatial design leaders come from diverse backgrounds, including film, acting, music, software development, architecture, hardware engineering, data science, motion graphics, graphic design, and UX design. This variety of experiences underscores the importance of thinking spatially and converging knowledge from different domains, highlighting the interdisciplinary nature of the field. Paul Hoover, Head of Design at ShapesXR, said "So no matter if you are a designer, artist, animator, filmmaker, developer or marketer, specialize in one skill first, you can use this skill to get in the door." And then learn 3D and prototype skills or coding skills. Similarly, Susan Cummings, CEO/Co-Founder of Tiny Rebel Games (creators of Petaverse), underlined the importance of versatility and a multidisciplinary approach for those aspiring to enter the industry. They also emphasized the value of experimentation and approaching games from a designer's perspective. Furthermore, Susan shared insights on the future of AR and VR technologies, envisioning them becoming more integrated and immersive, thereby transforming entertainment and gaming into more integral parts of our daily lives.

Thomas Van Bouwel, recognized for his contributions to Cubism and Laser Dance as a VR Developer, highlighted the evolving landscape of spatial design in the industry. He noted a shift towards smaller, more flexible teams within studios. This trend, according to Thomas, is largely driven by the increased accessibility and affordability of tools like Unity and Blender, coupled with a wealth of learning resources such as YouTube tutorials. In this streamlined environment, team members often wear multiple hats, contributing to various facets of a project. Thomas emphasized the importance of having multi-skilled professionals in this multimedia-centric field. He advocates for a balanced approach: specializing in one area while simultaneously developing a diverse skill set to navigate different forms of media effectively. Jason Marsh, CEO of Flow Immersive, recounted an impressive coding journey that started when he was just six years old. With over five decades of coding experience, Jason has observed the evolution of the technological landscape firsthand. Highlighting the continuing importance of technical knowledge in an age increasingly influenced by AI, Jason promotes a culture of curiosity and lifelong learning. He encourages individuals to eagerly acquire knowledge, ask questions without hesitation, and embrace the rapidly changing tech world with an open and inquisitive mindset.

Critical Thinking

In the dynamic realms of XR and spatial design, critical thinking emerges as an indispensable skill. It ignites innovative ideas, refines user experiences, and ensures that designs are not only aesthetically pleasing and easy to interact with, but also ethical, secure, and universally accessible.

Estella Tse, an XR Creative Director and Artist, highlighted that compelling storytelling does not require the use of immersive media. She pointed out the various mediums through which powerful narratives can be effectively conveyed, such as writing and painting. Estella stresses the significance of intentional design prior to undertaking a creative project, asking herself pivotal questions like: Why choose XR as the preferred medium? Does the narrative benefit qualitatively from XR? And does XR technology truly enhance the storytelling experience? These questions ensure that XR's utilization adds substantial value to the narrative, rather than merely being a technological gimmick.

Critical thinking is akin to a mental toolbox essential for decision-making. It's the process of objectively analyzing information to draw well-founded conclusions. When designing in spatial design, one might consider questions such as: Is a controller necessary? Do we need a large UI panel? Can we replace this interface with more innovative technology inputs? How can accessibility be enhanced? What options exist for users with limited mobility? Critical thinking encompasses valuable skills like reasoning, analysis, interpretation, and reflection. Imagine being a detective: collecting diverse clues, understanding the broader context, and posing key questions. It involves evaluating the credibility of information, identifying hidden biases or assumptions, and examining details to discern overarching patterns.

By applying logical reasoning, you assemble various pieces of information, consider different viewpoints, and understand cause-and-effect relationships. Critical thinking, a skill that can be sharpened with practice and feedback, is crucial as it enables informed decision-making and efficient problem-solving. Critical thinking is invaluable in seamlessly integrating various technologies, balancing creativity with practicality, and staying abreast of the constantly evolving tech landscape. It's about truly understanding user needs, boldly facing technological challenges, and addressing complex ethical dilemmas. Ultimately, critical thinking is the key to creating exceptional, user-centric designs in these rapidly progressing fields.

Resilience

Estella Tse believes that resilience is the key trait for anyone in spatial design. With the rapid pace of technological and tool updates, finding answers online can be a real challenge. Often, she finds herself piecing together various tutorials and resources, experimenting to see what works. The constant introduction of new technologies, SDKs, and APIs can be overwhelming and sometimes frustrating. She recalls spending days figuring out issues like texture and model compatibility or performance optimization. It's this resilience, the willingness to try, fail, and experiment with new technologies, that really makes the difference. In a field that's always evolving, being adaptable and having a strong problem-solving mindset, coupled with the courage to embrace failure, are invaluable qualities.

Conclusion

The designer revolution encapsulates the transformative journey of design roles and responsibilities in the era of spatial AI and XR technologies. From the evolution of job duties that transition from specialized tasks to a holistic approach to problem-solving to the shift from specialist to generalist roles encompassing a wide array of disciplines, this revolution in design signifies a paradigm shift. It's not just about being adept in traditional design skills, but also about embracing the complexities of 3D environments, AI, and technology, and understanding the nuances of business and policy. The journey from graphic design to UX, UX to XR, and ultimately spatial design, illustrates the expanding scope and depth of a designer's role.

Designers today are expected to be versatile, with a strong foundation in critical thinking and resilience. They must navigate through constant technological advancements, adapt to new tools, and continually refine their skills in storytelling, user experience, and interactive design. This revolution is not just about tools and technologies; it's about the mindset. It's about understanding the impact of design on the user experience, the ethical considerations of AI and technology, and the importance of creating accessible and inclusive designs. It's about looking at design not just to create visually appealing products but to craft experiences that are meaningful, engaging, and transformative. As we embrace this new era of design, we are challenged to think beyond conventional boundaries, innovate, and create designs that are not only functional and aesthetically pleasing but also intuitive, empathetic, and responsive to the needs of an increasingly complex and interconnected world. This is the essence of the designer revolution – a shift towards a more integrated, comprehensive, and human-centered approach to design.

3

Ten Spatial Design Principles

*"The broader one's understanding of the human experience,
the better design we will have."*
–Steve Jobs

In *A Pattern Language*,[7] Christopher Alexander presents a comprehensive set of design concepts known as patterns, forming a cohesive language. He explains, "*All 253 patterns together form a language*," highlighting the interconnectedness of these designs. Each pattern tackles a specific issue, offering a solution, and thus systematizing the approach to common design challenges. Drawing inspiration from Christopher Alexander, *The Ten Spatial Design Principles* are presented with overarching guidelines for "Why", "What", and "How". Correspondingly, the key design patterns, aligned with each principle, are inherently flexible, permitting restructuring and combination to forge a unique language. They act as versatile building blocks, readily available for creative assembly. The Ten Design Principles and Key Design Patterns serve as a foundational aid in crafting exceptional spatial designs. This chapter presents a top-down approach, starting with the question "Why is this important". Then, explaining "what it is about". And finally, describing how to make using examples. "The how to" on the bottom is the concrete plan for "how to build a solution". We'll present each design principle in this chapter in sections describing **why**, **what**, and **how**. At the end of each section, a table will summarize the design patterns as building blocks, which can be used to create a unique language. This is the bottom-up approach.

---

[7] Christopher Alexander, *A Pattern Language, 1977.*

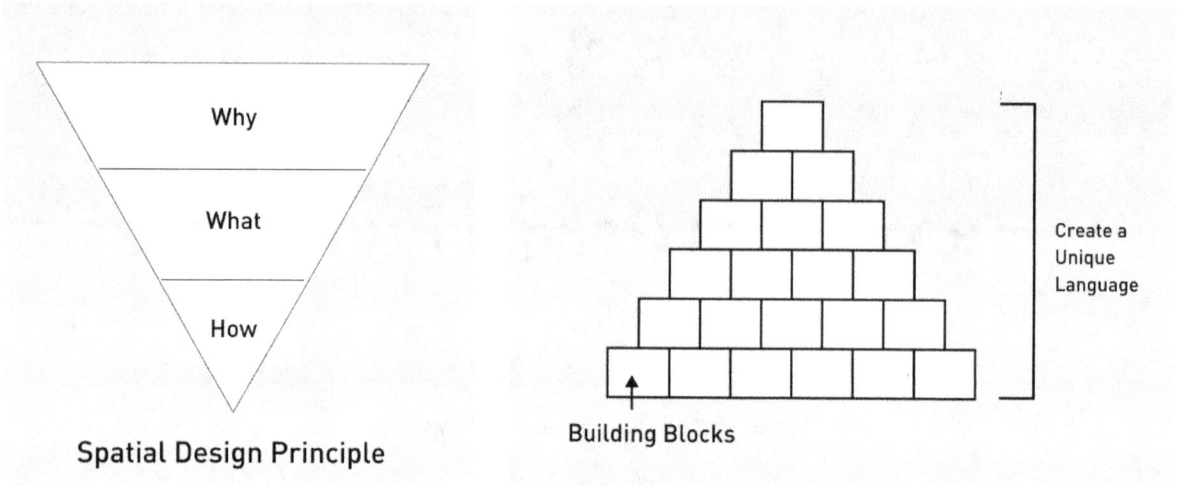

Fig. 3.1: The Ten Spatial Design Principles are presented with overarching guidelines for "Why", "What", and "How" in a top-down approach (Left). Bottom-Up Key design patterns, aligned with each principle, are inherently flexible, permitting restructuring and combination to forge a unique language. They act as versatile building blocks, readily available for creative assembly (Right).

For professionals in spatial design, understanding foundational technologies and user interaction is just the beginning. It's crucial to rapidly transform concepts into tangible prototypes. Spatial design is inherently interdisciplinary, requiring a comprehensive grasp of experience design, technology, and 3D modeling to create immersive experiences. When developing spatial design products, the mental and physical interactions of the user with the product are key considerations.

Furthermore, spatial design often involves collecting extensive user data such as room scans, iris recognition, body movements, eye tracking, gestures, and voice commands. This requires the creation of a secure environment to safeguard user information, pushing spatial designers to extend their focus beyond just interaction and interface design. In the blog *The Laws of Simplicity Applied to VR*,[8] Paulo Melchiori reflects on how Dr. John Maeda's book influenced his approach to leading the VR OS design team. And the ten spatial design principles were inspired by the blog.

---

[8] Paulo Melchiori, The Laws of Simplicity applied to VR, https://uxdesign.cc/the-laws-of-simplicity-applied-to-vr-87418ec34aa4, accessed Jan 2023.

Here are the ten spatial design principles:

10 Spatial Design Principles

Fig. 3.2: Illustration of the Ten Spatial Design Principles

1. **Engage:** Capturing and holding attention often sparks a profound, personal feeling, creating unforgettable experiences.
2. **Innovate:** People expect the spatial design experience to be new and original.
3. **Diversity:** Diversity, equity, and inclusion (DEI) in spatial design.
4. **Context:** Enrich user experience, seamlessly blending virtual elements with reality, ensuring user safety and accessibility and relevant content.
5. **Connect:** Connect people to create meaningful experiences.
6. **Comfort:** Comfort in spatial design contributes to a more immersive experience.
7. **Reduce:** Less is more, so keep it simple.
8. **Personalize:** Customize the experience for individual needs.
9. **Evaluate:** Users can get feedback from their actions.
10. **Safe:** Create a physically and psychologically safe experience for everyone.

Engage

Key Design Patterns:

1. **Storytelling:** Craft a compelling narrative that resonates with your audience. Use storytelling to create a connection between the user and the experience.

2. **Immersive Design:** Design environments and interactions that are immersive and realistic, enhancing the user's sense of presence in the world.

3. **Interactive Elements:** Incorporate interactive elements that allow users to feel like active participants rather than passive observers.

4. **Emotion-Driven Audio:** Use sound and music effectively to evoke emotions and set the tone.

5. **Sensory Engagement:** Engage multiple senses (sight, sound, touch) to create a more holistic experience.

6. **Show, Don't Tell:** If you can show it, don't describe it. Try to use the natural way instead of explaining things. Reduce the tutorials and learn how to interact by making everything interactable.

Why is Engagement Important?

Have you ever experienced a live performance or a magic show that left a lasting impression? I recall the exhilarating experience of "The Void - Star Wars: Secrets of the Empire," where the surreal intensity of confronting Darth Vader face-to-face sent shivers down my spine. This was akin to the thrill I felt during my high school trip, attending the live performance of "Phantom of the Opera" in London. The chandelier's dramatic fall and the distinct smell of gunpowder during the battle scenes are vivid in my mind. Such immersive experiences are important—they make us feel alive. It's the spectrum of emotions—excitement, happiness, sorrow, anger, fear, and joy—that make our existence meaningful.

What is Engagement?

A good immersive experience should allow the user to enter the "Flow" state; in which the user or player focuses on the tasks without being distracted. Mihaly Csikszentmihalyi, a pioneer in the field of positive psychology, describes the elusive state of flow as when we feel fully in control, exhilarated, and deeply engaged in our actions—a benchmark for an ideal life.[9]

At the ShapesXR & XReality Pro TableTop hackathon, Paul Hoover, the head designer at ShapesXR, introduced three pivotal judging criteria: Emotional Impact, Authenticity, and Narratives. Rather than centering on technical aspects like game polish or mechanics, these criteria emphasize a return to the fundamental essence of what makes us human. This approach underscores the importance of engaging emotions, genuine storytelling, and authenticity in design over mere technical prowess.

Products like Supernatural and Beat Saber excel at delivering this state by using intuitive mechanics, minimalistic design, and a gradual progression of difficulty levels to keep players challenged but able to progress to new accomplishments. Real-time feedback and physical engagement trigger endorphins, enhancing both enjoyment and well-being during gameplay and keeping users coming back for more.

In spatial design experiences, we simulate the environment and trigger emotion more than in traditional 2D experiences, while reducing the distractions. The key to achieving flow hinges on the user being able to progress through a journey of incremental milestones, rather than simply engaging in passive activities. Successful implementation

---

[9] Csikszentmihalyi, Mihaly (1990). "Flow: The Psychology of Optimal Experience"

of this flow state will keep users free from distractions and completely immersed in what they are doing.

Spatial design offers an incredibly immersive experience, serving as a powerful medium for storytelling that etches enduring memories. These memorable moments enrich our lives with meaning and wonder, showcasing the profound impact of immersive experiences on our perception and emotions.

How to Create Engagement in Spatial Design?

Immerse Yourself in the Environment

"I was sitting on a beanbag, experiencing the world from the perspective of fungi at the forest floor, and was overwhelmed with a deeply peaceful awareness of the interconnectedness of all life forms in nature." - Karen Stritzinger, Founder of Old Hara Studios on her experience with Forager[10]

Karen mentioned her favorite recent experience is the VR app *How to Rescue a Reef*,[11] created by the University of Miami for Meta Quest. This immersive app allows users to embody a marine scientist working to rejuvenate a dying coral reef, skillfully using immersive technology to inspire real-world action and solutions. Equally impactful for her was the VR experience *Forager*, which shifts focus from direct scientific action to restoring our emotional bond with nature. In Forager, users are transported to the forest floor, adopting the perspective of fungi. She was deeply impressed by the designers' ability to engage all senses, creating a truly transformative experience.

For Karen, the most significant potential of content to enhance public awareness and climate action lies not just in visualizing impacts, but more so in enabling people to

---

[10] Porter, Winslow, Forager, https://www.forager.earth, accessed Jan. 2024.
[11] University of Miami (2023). "How to Rescue a Reef". https://rescueareef.earth.miami.edu, accessed Jan. 2024.

envision the future we aspire to create. Understanding and conceptualizing solutions is crucial, as we cannot strive for what we cannot imagine, especially when these solutions seem daunting. Spatial design offers a remarkable opportunity to raise awareness about the systemic roots of environmental issues and to highlight the progress made by inspiring activists, scientists, and businesses. By sharing these experiences across diverse geographic regions, spatial design facilitates global comprehension and collaboration in finding and implementing solutions.

Create Magic Moment and a Sense of Wonder

Spatial design technology offers a unique medium for creating experiences that defy the constraints of the physical world, akin to magic. In the Mixed-Reality game *Pillow*,[12] this concept is vividly brought to life. Here, the ceiling becomes a canvas for wonder, where users lying in bed can engage in activities like fishing projected onto it. This creates an enchanting illusion, so lifelike that it blurs the line between reality and fantasy, leaving players with a memorable experience that lingers long after the game is over.

As for VR live theater, it is a burgeoning genre that seems perfectly suited for immersive theater, emphasizing interaction, intimacy, and immersion. The art form becomes accessible beyond physical locations, enabling audiences to enjoy these stories from their homes using VR headsets.

---

[12] Rizzotto, Lucas. https://www.pillow.social, accessed Jan. 2024.

Fig. 3.3: Deirdre took on the role of Onyx, an elderly alien who enlisted the player's aid to complete three quests, each unlocking a portion of her power source. (Source: Deirdre V. Lyons)

Deirdre V. Lyons, Co-Founder at Ferryman Collective, unveiled "Gumball Dreams"[13] in VRChat, co-created with Screaming Color (aka Christopher Lane Davis), which is an immersive live theater experience. The production was a feast for the senses, with a brilliant fusion of colors and a boundless spatial canvas that showcased creativity and the realization of the impossible. The intimate theater setup for three participants began with Deirdre embodying an AI robot avatar, guiding attendees through initial interactions by having them manipulate game elements and adjust VRChat settings.

This introductory phase, facilitated by the robot Deirdre played, was designed for ease and learning. As the experience progressed, participants encountered the main character, a venerable blue alien also portrayed by Deirdre named Onyx, who sought assistance in recharging her energy through a trio of inventive missions. Each mission presented a unique creative challenge reminiscent of 'The Legend of Zelda's shrine puzzles,' culminating in uplifting messages for the players. Upon completion of the tasks, Onyx led the group skyward to the apex of the sky dome, where the expansiveness of

Fig. 3.4: There are some puzzles for the players to get to the key. Beams of light will shoot down from above. (Source: Deirdre V. Lyons)

---

[13] Gumball Dreams (2022), https://www.ferrymancollective.com/gumball-dreams, Jan. 2024.

the earlier setting was now a miniature creation beneath them. Onyx encapsulated the essence of the experience by affirming that we are architects of our own mindscape, capable of turning dreams into reality.

The adventure concluded with the ascension of Onyx, in a chosen transition of this life to the next. This spectacular ending, coupled with the entire experience, which included an ethereal dive into an infinite ocean, where the players were enveloped by schools of fish and a kaleidoscope of exotic, colorful lights, created an overall experience symbolizing the limitless potential of imagination and creativity.

Delightful Headset Experience

"You need to make the experience delightful and worth it for people to get into the headset." - John Hanacek, XR Interaction Designer at Nanome Inc

John emphasizes the importance of creating experiences that are engaging and fulfilling, to make the use of headsets a rewarding choice for users. Rather than just gamifying applications in an arbitrary way to stave off boredom and fatigue, he advocates for enlivening professional apps in a way that keeps users engaged.

Integrating direct manipulation, distant interaction, and even playful gestures into the VR experience can transform activities that are frustrating to do on 2D computers into obvious and enjoyable activities. The aim is to enrich professional duties with a sense of agency that resonates with the users' goals, offering them a fresh and engaging perspective in their field. This method is designed to captivate and motivate users, prompting them to dive in and interact directly, thereby converting potential hindrances into sources of amusement and elevating their professional endeavors. The essence of spatial design lies in crafting such experiences, moving beyond the confines of flat, 2D interfaces to immersive, 3D interactions. This initiative is focused on bringing joy to the user's workflow, ensuring that putting on a headset becomes an enticing and pleasurable choice.

Furthermore, John notes the necessity of understanding the technical aspects and capabilities that technology affords for design. Specific hardware and software combinations yield different results, and all come with real-world tradeoffs that need balancing. Choosing the incorrect target and/or framework can be detrimental, hence, a robust technical understanding of the entire XR technology stack through hands-on experience enhances design quality, especially for non-technical individuals. For the technically adept, it's advised not to confine oneself to just one framework but to be versatile and efficient, learning to demonstrate capabilities through action rather than mere explanation.

Create a Playful Experience

Kyle Morrand, CEO at 302 Interactive, integrated his "Playful Experience" philosophy into spatial design, moving away from traditional gamification and emphasizing goals and win/lose states. This approach is particularly beneficial for non-game sector applications, focusing on the intrinsic joy of play without the pressure of objectives or competition. Being playful is distinct from engaging in a game. A game is structured around objectives and regulations, whereas being playful embodies a sense of unadulterated delight that isn't contingent on adhering to rules or achieving victory.

A prime example of this approach is showcased in the *Verapy Therapy*[14] case study on 302 Interactive's website. As a play consultant and development partner, Kyle and his team focused on creating a Virtual Reality platform designed to engage children in physical therapy exercises through game-like experiences. The process involved a thorough "Play Audit," assessing the platform's UX design and game design.

Collaborating with Verapy, the team at 302 Interactive developed new user flows, wireframes, and mockups, envisioning an enhanced version of the platform. This phase was followed by rapid prototyping, demonstrating the technical feasibility of the proposed concepts. Ultimately, the application of "Playful Experience" by 302 Interactive

---

[14] 302 Interactive, https://www.302interactive.com/verapy-therapy-a-case-study, accessed Jan 2024.

resulted in significant improvements for clients, including long-term patient retention, enhanced short-term patient engagement, easy-to-use solutions for therapists, and data-driven tools. These tools not only streamline therapy processes but also enable therapists to conduct more empathetic assessments of their patients.

Created an Engaging Experience with the Users

In *Hyper-Reality, The Art of Designing Impossible Experiences,*[15] author Curtis Hickman explores the nuances of storytelling in immersive environments. He advocates for showing rather than telling in these experiences, acknowledging that users often overlook voiceovers and descriptions upon entering a virtual world. Hickman identifies this phenomenon as *Media Apathy,*[16] where guests may not fully engage with the narrative of a theme park or similar setting. The emphasis is on interaction over narration, creating a digital environment that is responsive and contextually aware, enhancing the user experience.

When developing the Ghostbuster experience for Sony, Curtis and his team prioritized what they most desired to experience as Ghostbusters, such as getting slimed by Slimer and causing widespread property destruction with a proton stream, among other exciting scenarios. Curtis' approach deviates from traditional script-first methods.[17] He and his team prioritize the desired emotional responses and experiences of the audience.

Drawing inspiration from detective and mystery fiction, particularly the roles outlined by Robert J. Ray in *The Weekend Novelist Writes a Mystery*, Curtis modified and reapplied these archetypes - the Sleuth, Killer, Victim, and Catalyst - to spatial design. These

---

[15] Hickman Curtis, Hyper-Reality: The Art of Designing Impossible Experiences, KDP Paperback Edition 1.1, Las Vegas, NA.

[16] Hickman Curtis, Hyper-Reality: The Art of Designing Impossible Experiences, page 54. KDP Paperback Edition 1.1, Las Vegas, NA.

[17] Hickman Curtis, Hyper-Reality: The Art of Designing Impossible Experiences, page 66-67. KDP Paperback Edition 1.1, Las Vegas, NA.

roles are central to pivotal scenes in mystery narratives, such as the Killing Scene, Discovery of the Corpse, and Crime Scene.

In the realm of spatial design, user engagement can vary greatly. It ranges from high engagement, where users co-create the story through extensive interaction, to low engagement, where they simply enjoy the creator's narrative with minimal involvement. Users can embody different roles: as a 'Witness,' they observe without influencing the story; as a 'Victim,' they feel the story's impact without control; as a 'Sleuth,' they have the capacity to change the narrative indirectly; and as a 'Killer,' they actively shape and are shaped by the story. These roles provide a broad spectrum of experiences in spatial design, from passive observation to active participation, thus diversifying and enriching the immersive experience.[18]

Immersive Data Visualization

Jason Marsh, CEO of Flow Immersive, spoke about the mission of his company, which utilizes XR to communicate data through storytelling. He shared some data numbers about climate changes on a 2D screen which failed to convey the seriousness of the problem. But when the data is in 3 dimensions in the room, it changes the user's perspective, and they feel a sense of urgency. He pinpointed the oversimplification of data as a significant business challenge, which spurred him to develop a solution aimed at improving credibility and comprehension among business executives.

Fig. 3.5: Flow Immersive uses AI to visualize the data on a 3D radar chart and how to extract specific information related to a particular data point. (Source: Flow Immersive)

[18] Hickman Curtis, Hyper-Reality: The Art of Designing Impossible Experiences, page 108. KDP Paperback Edition 1.1, Las Vegas, NA.

Fig. 3.6: Flow Immersive uses AI to visualize the data so the team can feel the data through data visualization. (Source: Flow Immersive)

Flow Immersive addresses this challenge by constructing interactive, spatial, and narrative-focused shared mental models of data. This method not only bolsters credibility and understanding but also grants users a greater sense of expertise and command over the information.

The platform is designed for multi-user interaction, fostering collaboration between experts and non-experts, and enhancing engagement through immersive storytelling. Jason showcased a use case involving temperature anomaly data in the northern hemisphere, focusing on land temperatures, and demonstrating data filtering, viewing, and AI-powered 3D radar chart visualization. This case highlighted an anomaly in September and illustrated how the technology provides both detailed and big-picture insights.

Put Yourself in Someone's Shoes by Role Play

Ruth Diaz, Co-founder at inPath XR, has introduced several hundred worlds in Meta Horizon Worlds, designed to enlighten, inspire, and cultivate empathy among creators, community members, and the world. One of the worlds is "DACA: Plane Public Demo" - Pathway for Under-Recognized Folks created by the InPath XR team, including Ruth. In this intentionally designed immersive experience, participants start seated in an airplane, tasked with filling out a "U.S. Customs and Border Protection" form.

Fig. 3.8: In the immersive experience "DACA: Plane Public Demo" - Pathway for Under-Recognized Folks, players begin by sitting in an airplane seat. This setting is designed to help players empathize with individuals under the DACA program, offering a firsthand perspective on their experiences. (Resource: Ruth Diaz)

They are guided through a series of events mirroring the experiences of individuals under the Deferred Action for Childhood Arrivals (DACA) program. One scenario involves being taken to an office for investigation, leading to detention. This virtual journey is crafted to deepen a person's understanding and empathy for those affected by DACA programs.

Ruth possesses an extraordinary talent for building worlds on purpose, which is Ruth, a human on purpose, whose goal is to enable individuals to truly see themselves. Each of Ruth's numerous worlds weaves a narrative journey super filled with depth and meaning, immersing you not only into the virtual realms but also into emotions and sensations that you may not have known existed and not experienced with such depth and beauty. There's no going back, and you wouldn't want to. Onward we traveled into the depths of VR to a world simply titled, "Mirror." This world is an educational experience, enlightening individuals about the concept of 'Trolling' in the virtual world through a carefully curated array of diverse and insightful scenes of trolling. This world empowers individuals to truly understand and consider the effects of trolling on others (and what's happening sometimes underneath).

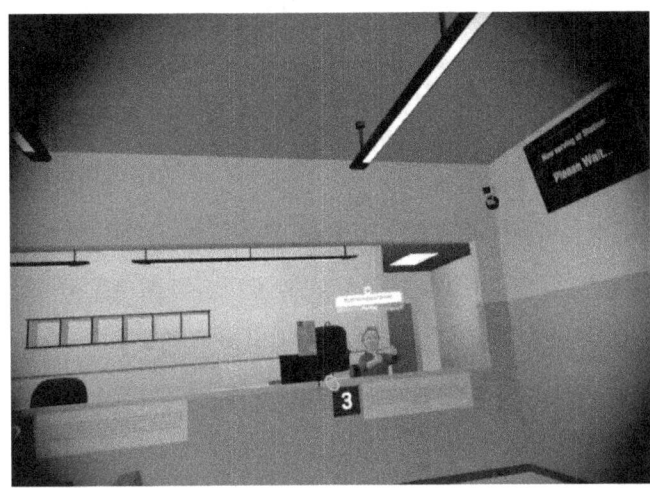

Fig. 3.7: Players were able to experience how people under DACA went through the procedure of getting through customs. (Source: Ruth Diaz)

Ruth has spotlighted a VR experience available on Quest 2 that replicates the visual perspective of individuals who are blind or have low vision. Designed to cultivate empathy and insight into their world perception, "Notes on Blindness"[19] serves as a powerful example. This immersive game explores the story of John Hull, who became blind in 1983. It uses Hull's own audio diaries to provide an intimate view into the reality of blindness, artfully combining storytelling, a unique graphical environment, motion tracking, spatialized audio, and interactive gameplay. Ruth shared her experience working with a legally blind VR user named Tony, who dreamed of creating a world where they could interact with a whale. Ruth and her team worked to make the UI user-friendly for Tony, but they did not make enough progress. However, they were able to improve their experience by adjusting the contrast of the environmental setting, allowing them to navigate a larger space. Ruth also created a box called Tony's Box, which simulated Tony's blindness and helped developers empathize with their experience.

Size, Layout, and Arrangement Change Our Perspectives

The scale of objects within the same space can significantly influence the emotional engagement in an experience. Ruth's Environmental Design mentor, Don Carson, illustrated this concept using a sphere in a room. A smaller-sized sphere was perceived as approachable, whereas a larger sphere in the same room evoked a sense of oppression. This demonstrates how object size can impact the emotional response and engagement level in an environment.

---

[19] Notes on Blindness, https://www.arte.tv/digitalproductions/en/notes-on-blindness, accessed Jan. 2024

Engagement-Driven Visual, Gamified, and Audio

Tripp,[20] a VR app available on the Meta Store, offers a "mindful metaverse" with personalized virtual experiences tailored to enhance relaxation and mindfulness. Users can access a range of meditative content, teachings, and immersive worldscapes, with the flexibility to customize duration and focus areas, such as calming the mind or deepening self-connection. It uses emotional visuals, simplicity, and soothing music, voiceover teaching to help people relax.

Building Blocks for Engagement

Components:	Actions:
Storytelling	• Craft a compelling narrative that resonates with your audience.
A Sense of Wonder	• Create a world that leaves players with memorable experiences.
Role Playing	• See the world from someone's unique perspective.
Immersion for the Senses	• Visual, audio, and spatial environments that captivate and focus the user's attention.
Interactive Elements	• Incorporate interactive elements

---

[20] Tripp is a VR wellness meditation product that provides personalized meditation and mindfulness journeys, acclaimed for its innovative approach. Tripp has received awards like Best Meditation App 2023 and Best Inventions of 2022. Official website: https://www.tripp.com

Innovate

"The true sign of intelligence is not knowledge but imagination."
–Albert Einstein

Key Design Patterns:

1. **Rapid Prototyping:** The faster you can see the experience from concept to realization, the more innovative this project can be.

2. **Constant Feedback from Users:** Get as much feedback from the users and adjust the design and development ASAP to make sure the ideas meet reality.

3. **Learn from Everyday Life:** Accelerate the production pipeline by simultaneously fostering ideation and creation.

4. **No-Code Prototype and AI:** Speed up the production pipeline, ideation and creation happens at the same time.

5. **Combine Interests and Different Fields of Expertise:** Creativity is all about connecting the dots. So go out and explore your own interests and collaborate with subject matter experts.

6. **Rule-Breaker:** Learn the rules and then break them. The best spatial experience is from those who break the rules.

7. **Share Ideas on Social Media for Validation:** The quality of an app isn't determined by adhering to rules but rather by the judgment of its users.

Why is Innovation Important?

People have high expectations for the virtual environment to be innovative, the environment can be anything and beyond your imagination. Lorelle VanFossen, Director of Educators in VR, shared insights into audience engagement in digital twin virtual environments. Most clients wish to emulate the real world by creating digital twins. She noted that initially, visitors to digital twin worlds brought fascination. "This is just like the real world." Subsequent visits brought yawns and a "been there, done that" response. Participants often commented "this is VR so we can go anywhere!"

This flexibility and capacity for creativity is a fundamental reason why virtual worlds captivate so many people. So, keep "surprising" us with innovative creative ideas, something that we have never seen before, where the imagination becomes reality!

What is Innovative in Spatial Design?

In the realm of XR and spatial computing, technology is rapidly evolving, continuously integrating with other technologies daily. Due to its technological adaptability, which embraces constant updates and innovation, spatial design possesses immense potential for pioneering advancements. These experiences showcase the boundless innovation at the intersection of the physical and virtual worlds, layering reality upon reality and offering roles in diverse, fantastical domains that fuel our innate desire for creativity.

How to Innovate in Spatial Design?

Rapid Prototyping

Thomas Van Bouwel, VR Developer on Cubism & Laser Dance, said that the way to create a good game is to come up with a quick prototype within 1-2 days, then share it to social media and see how the audience responds. If the response is positive, then continue. If not, make quick changes and share it on social media for feedback.

Constantly Get Feedback from Users

Thomas shared his process of working on the user testing for the mixed reality game "Laser Dance". He attended in-person events and gatherings popular with families to collect player feedback. These sessions revealed a vast diversity in height, age, body shape, gender, and flexibility among players, all of whom tried out the game. Based on feedback, he implemented numerous customizations to enhance the gaming experience. He also requested that testers upload 3D scanning of their rooms, enabling him to swiftly simulate the game's mixed-reality environment within Unity. This process ensured that the game's settings were adaptable to a wide array of real-world scenarios. Such hands-on testing allowed him to innovate while remaining grounded in practical application.

Get Inspirations from Everyday Life

Thomas is enthusiastic about the potential of mixed reality to revolutionize interaction methods. He views his home as a vast new interface and canvas ripe for innovative interactions. Drawing inspiration from building blocks, he swiftly leveraged social media to gather feedback for his project *Cubism*.[21]

Cubism stands out for its minimalistic approach to user interactions in mixed reality. While playable on a desktop, it truly shines as a 3D puzzle game that evokes memories of Tetris, enhanced by an elegant musical score. The game's objective is to assemble complex structures from colorful blocks, with the difficulty increasing as players advance. This game is particularly engaging due to its simple yet thoughtful design.

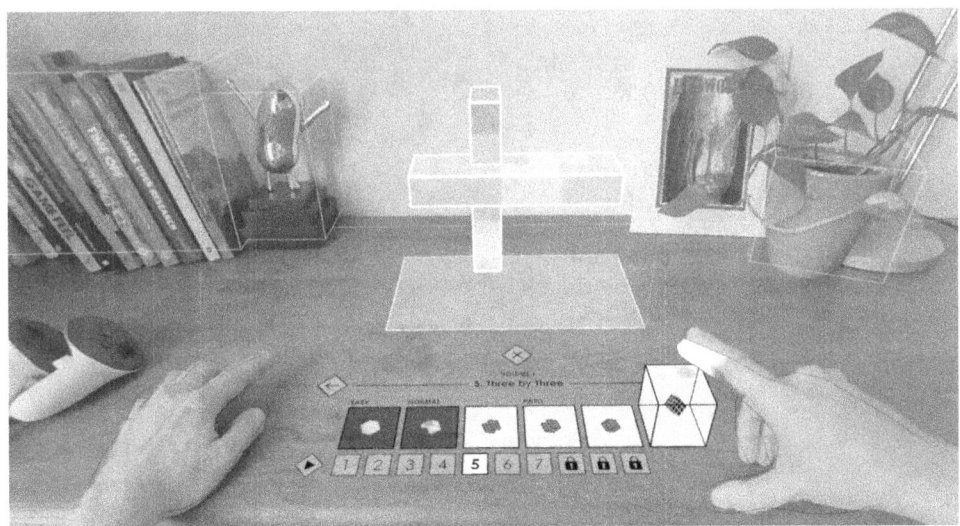

---

[21] Cubism, https://www.cubism-vr.com, accessed Jan. 2024

Paul Hoover, head designer at ShapesXR, explains that the virtual world design for multiple players and users is like architecture and city planning. People have many needs in an environment. For example, in the workplace, people want to be social, collaborate and work alone. In the real-world office setup, a normal office has a place to hang out, eat food, presentation, and a private place to work alone. In the virtual world, in multiplayer design, people also want to hang out, or present themselves as more formal and collaborate with each other while working privately in their personal space. In ShapesXR, the avatar color indicates whether a user is on the same stage/page as others during presentation and same page modes. If a user is not aligned with others, their avatar turns gray. In presentation mode, avatars are hidden to maintain focus on the showcased design. Additionally, user representation alternates between a full-body avatar and a headset icon based on the user's scale. In 'God's mode', where the user significantly enlarges, the avatar switches to a headset icon to avoid obstructing the environment and the design.

Addressing Industry Challenges with Spatial Computing

"Creativity is just connecting things. When you ask creative people how they did something, they feel a little guilty because they didn't really do it, they just saw something. It seemed obvious to them after a while." —Steve Jobs

Spatial computing is not just a tool, it serves as a vital visualization tool that

Fig. 3.10: In ShapesXR, people can work alone or collaboratively, in the same space or not in the same space. (Source: ShapesXR and XReality Pro hackathon event)

requires meaningful content to reach its full potential. Simply showcasing the technology without relevant content may result in providing little value to the audience, turning it into nothing more than a superficial distraction.

According to Damon Hernandez, CEO of Mixx Reality, a promising approach is to merge your specific interests with spatial computing to initiate innovative projects. For instance, within the realm of spatial computing and XR, individuals with backgrounds in architecture have crafted astonishing virtual world and space design experiences. Similarly, those with expertise in health and medicine can leverage spatial computing technologies to develop innovative solutions, such as training programs and visualizations to help patients understand medical procedures better.

Moreover, for individuals passionate about fields like cooking, music, and clothing design, integrating these diverse disciplines into the spatial computing landscape can ignite innovative possibilities. The most groundbreaking applications in spatial computing often emerge when different fields come together to address real-world challenges. For example, Nanome offers innovative solutions that facilitate real-time collaboration in molecular design using virtual reality, spanning from general chemistry to pharmaceutical drug discovery. Another noteworthy mention is SENTIO VR, the premier immersive cloud platform for reviewing designs, managing client presentations, and fostering collaboration among professionals in the building industry. Both companies exemplify the successful fusion of spatial computing and XR with various domains, showcasing the transformative potential of this interdisciplinary approach.

Using No-Code Prototype Tools to Quickly Build and Test

In Horizon Worlds, creators have the innovative ability to scale their avatars up for grand-scale world editing or shrink down to experience the environment as users would. This process transcends real-world limitations, where altering one's size to gain a macro or micro perspective is not possible. Such a feature enhances the development and testing phases, offering a unique approach to world-building. Prototype tools such as

ShapesXR have a similar function which allows the creators to quickly see and test out the ideas in virtual space, reducing the friction of production.

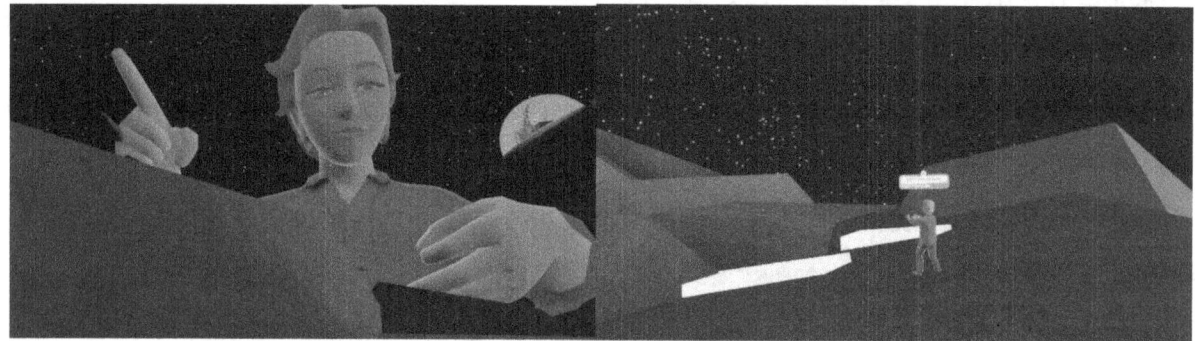

Fig. 3.11: In Horizon Worlds, creators can scale up to create the world while shrinking yourself down to test the world build, quickly ideate and test the experience without friction. (Source: Ruth Diaz)

Unlimited Opportunities: Create Beyond Reality

Spatial design opens a door to impossible experiences, enabling people to immerse themselves in scenarios beyond their everyday reach. In VRChat, you have the freedom to embody anything from a diminutive chicken to a colossal monster. Ruth Diaz has crafted a world named "Build Your Own Monster" within Horizon Worlds. This inventive space is brimming with creative elements—varied shapes for body parts, appendages, eyes, and accessories—allowing players to leap prodigiously, without physical constraints. The monsters we created were incredibly imaginative, surpassing anything we could create in the physical world.

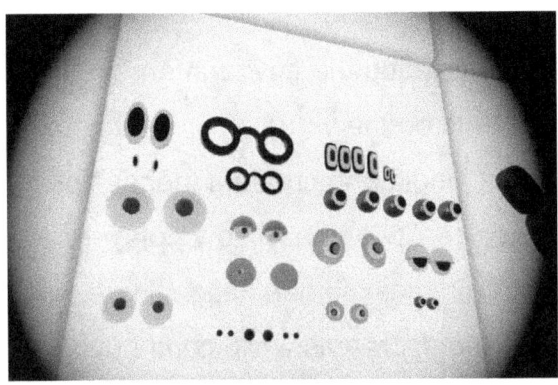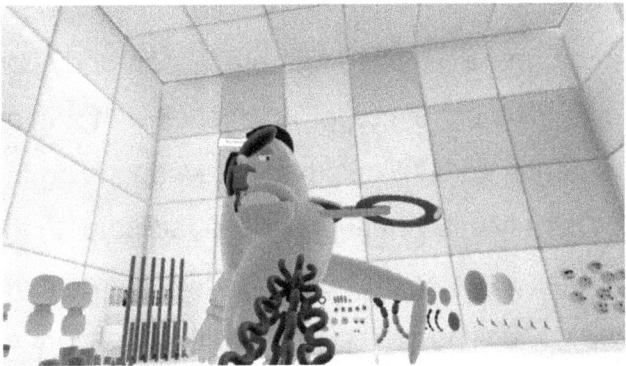

Fig. 3.12: All the eyeballs and different elements of creating monsters are on the virtual walls inside the room (Left). In VR, it allows players to go beyond the physical boundary and create something that would not be possible in real-life (Right). (Source: Ruth Diaz)

John Hanacek drew parallels between the early stages of film and the current phase of XR and spatial computing. He noted that initially, early motion camera users explored the potential of their medium with direct captures of reality. Later artists revolutionized it with storytelling and innovations like montage to create a cinematic language becoming truly a new medium. XR is similarly poised for a transformative leap where it develops its own native medium characteristics that are not possible to express in any other medium and are perhaps unimaginable without the new medium. Adding a touch of humor, he advised against mere replication in virtual experiences, using the Department of Motor Vehicles (DMV) as an example: "Don't just recreate the dull chairs and long lines typical of the DMV because that's how it's done in the world today. Our goal is to improve upon, not replicate all the tedious aspects of existing in the physical world. We can free ourselves from the constraints of the physical world while bringing in the best aspects of it when appropriate for grounding to craft more intentional, effective, and original virtual experiences and places. This early on is the best chance to free our minds and reinvent what we want to experience and find ideal expressions as we design virtual experiences."

Learn From Nature, Animals, and the Real-World

In the game "Gorilla Tag," players embody gorillas, navigating the environment on all fours. The act of propelling oneself with arm movements on the virtual floor delivers an authentic gorilla-like experience—bounding through a jungle and creating friendships in ways only this virtual realm can facilitate. In the mixed-reality game "Pillow", players lie on their beds as the ceiling and walls transform into a canvas of imagination. Here, one can go "ceiling fishing," capturing fishes that reveal others' dreams while contributing to this dreamscape by recording and releasing their own into this aerial pond.

The Best Games are Rule-Breakers: Let the Market Decide Best Practice

"Rules are for the obedience of fools and the guidance of wise men."
–Douglas Bader

Lee Vermeulen, CEO at Alientrap, emphasized that the market should decide on the best practices, noting that guidelines and rules from companies or academics can be limiting. They used the example of VR games, where common wisdom suggested not moving the camera, but popular games like Gorilla Tag moved the camera extensively. There are a lot of platform regulations due to easy to review the submissions, those are great to check and learn. But sometimes great VR games break the rules and patterns. Rapid user testing, integrating new technologies and innovations, and learning from the user testing, let the market decide the best practice.

Building Blocks for Innovation:

Components:	Actions:
Rapid Prototyping	• Create a good game with a quick prototype within 1-2 days. Then share it on social media and see how the intended audience responds.
Constant Feedback	• Based on user feedback, implement changes to improve user experience.
Addressing Industry Challenges	• Tackling industry challenges by leveraging spatial computing technologies.
No-Code Prototype Tools	• Enhance the development and testing phases using No-Code tools such as ShapesXR.
Real World Examples	• Learn from nature and real-world examples.
Let the Market Decide	• The market should decide on best practices.

Diversity

"I have a dream that my four little children will one day live in a nation where they will not be judged by the color of their skin but by the content of their character."
— *Martin Luther King Jr.*

Key Design Patterns:

1. **Inclusive User Interface Design:** Designing user interfaces that are easy to navigate and understand for people from different cultural and linguistic backgrounds. This might involve multilingual support and intuitive symbols that transcend language barriers.

2. **Accessibility Features:** Implementing features that cater to users with disabilities, such as voice commands for users with motor impairments, visual aids for users with hearing impairments, or screen readers for visually impaired users.

3. **Gender Inclusivity:** Avoiding gender stereotypes in the design of XR environments and characters. This includes providing non-binary gender options for avatars and ensuring that interactions within XR environments are respectful and inclusive of all gender identities.

4. **Socioeconomic Considerations:** Making XR technologies accessible to people from a range of socioeconomic backgrounds. This could involve developing scalable solutions that work on lower-end hardware or offering free or affordable access to certain XR applications, especially those with educational or practical value.

5. **Diverse Representation:** Design avatars, environments, and narratives that represent a wide range of cultures, identities, and abilities. This involves consulting with diverse groups during the development process.

6. **Accessibility and Inclusivity:** Ensure the technology is accessible to users with different abilities and socioeconomic backgrounds.

7. **Inclusive Interaction:** Develop guidelines and moderation tools to foster respectful and inclusive interactions among users.

8. **Ongoing Evaluation:** Continuously monitor and update policies and practices to address emerging DEI concerns and security threats in the evolving digital landscape.

9. **Empower Women in Spatial Design**: Advancing women in spatial design requires educational initiatives, community support, leadership opportunities, fair workplace practices, and global collaboration to ensure diversity and inclusion in the field.

Why is Diversity Important in Spatial Design?

XR and spatial computing technologies are especially at risk for the exclusion of people with disabilities based on their immersive nature. In one of the IEEE XR ethics and diversity standard reports, it stated *"... consider an adventure game with a sword-wielding hero. With a traditional 2D interface, a player might press a button to swing their sword; in an XR version, they might physically swing their controller, an act requiring much more physical dexterity. If the designers do not consider an accessible alternative, many disabled gamers would be excluded."* [22]

To create a great experience for everyone, diversity in spatial computing and XR development is essential. A diverse team brings varied perspectives, enhancing cultural sensitivity and user experience, fostering innovation, and broadening market appeal. This approach ensures that products are accessible to a wide range of users, addresses potential biases, and promotes ethical development. Moreover, diversity in the development team leads to better representation in virtual environments,

---

[22] Dylan Fox, IEEE.org, https://standards.ieee.org/wp-content/uploads/2022/04/Ethics_Diversity_Inclusion_Accessibility.pdf, accessed Jan. 2024.

contributing to a sense of belonging for users from all backgrounds and driving economic success for companies through more innovative and appealing products.

What is Diversity?

"Diversity is the art of thinking independently together."
- Malcolm Forbes

Diversity is defined as *"the practice or quality of including or involving people from a range of different social and ethnic backgrounds and of different genders, sexual orientations, etc."*[23] Diversity in spatial design is to ensure that these technologies are inclusive and accessible to a broad spectrum of users.

How to Build Diversity?

"It's important to recognize that diversity leads to more innovative, more productive outcomes . . .Treating everyone with dignity and equal pay keeps people loyal. Recognizing them and rewarding them for what they have done will make us all strive towards that same goal of equity in the workplace. I think it's important for us to recognize that this is not just checking the box. This is not just lip service. This is an important, significant, critical success factor for the future of work." –Mitra Best, PwC Partner & Technology Impact Leader [24]

Diversity in spatial design encompasses creating experiences that are inclusive and accessible to a broad spectrum of users. It involves designing for varied abilities, backgrounds, and preferences, ensuring accessibility for people with disabilities through adaptive controls and interfaces, and incorporating diverse cultural perspectives to avoid stereotypes. The approach also includes developing inclusive content and

---

[23] National Library of Medicine, https://www.ncbi.nlm.nih.gov/pmc/articles/PMC8962281/#CR1, accessed Jan. 2024
[24] Virbela, https://www.virbela.com/blog/dei-in-xr-how-to-facilitate-diverse-achievements, accessed Jan. 2024

interaction designs that cater to different languages, gender identities, and cultural norms, while addressing ethical considerations like bias in AI algorithms and user privacy. Additionally, it involves collaboration and co-creation with a diverse group of individuals, fostering innovative and universally accessible XR experiences.

Addressed (DEI) for All Spatial Design Development

Ruth Diaz mentioned the lack of diversity within a group, especially regarding gender and ethnicity in the XR/Tech industry. Men dominate in the industry. We should include more diversities to be involved in the development. Ruth proposed a system to rate gaming companies based on their diversity, equity, and inclusion (DEI) practices, suggesting that those with lower ratings could be incentivized through a calling in and out process to contribute to a fund for smaller companies to build more diverse and inclusive games.

Fig. 3.13: Ruth developed an immersive environment within Meta Horizon Worlds specifically for DEI learning. Utilizing the principles of gamification and the power of narrative sharing, her creation aims to enhance people's understanding of DEI's significance in an engaging and interactive way.

Ruth discussed the concept of disassociation, noting its ability to manifest in fantasy scenarios. She touched upon the popularity of immersive digital experiences, suggesting they offer therapeutic escapism, but can also be

Fig. 3.14: The immersive experience *Mirror* explores the mental mindset associated with trolling in the virtual environment, offering a unique perspective on the psychological dynamics of such behavior. (Source: Ruth Diaz)

problematic. She highlighted the importance of fostering empathy in digital environments and emphasized the role of developers in understanding the user experience. Ruth suggested that creating large, open spaces in digital environments leads to better team functionality and creativity. She concluded by mentioning the exploration of different kinds of identities to build empathy.

Design Accessibility for All

"Provide comparable experiences for all users. Give users control of their experience by providing them with various options for how to complete tasks and/or how to alter their XR environment to fit their needs or desires."
–Dylan Fox, Director of Operations for XR Access

Chris McNally, co-founder at iMcNally, was born with low vision. He leverages AI and mixed-reality headsets to enhance his navigation. He uses mixed-reality glasses with an AI assistant that alerts him to obstacles and adjusts contrast for improved visibility. His work primarily focuses on advancing low-vision capabilities through state-of-the-art technologies. In the next 5 to 20 years, these innovations are poised to significantly improve the lives of individuals with low vision. His approach incorporates augmented reality technologies along with smart glasses, haptics, spatial audio, and tactile interfaces. Key to his strategy are technologies like AI, which utilize machine learning, neural networks, and deep learning models.

Fig. 3.15: A normal person's vision depicts a kitchen (Left). The scene is viewed through Chris's vision (Right). (Source: Chris McNally)

Chris discussed the importance of maintaining consistency and simplicity in user interface design for people with low vision. He emphasized the need for feedback in multiple modes and the significance of adhering to established accessibility guidelines such as the WCAG.[25] Chris highlighted the necessity of continuously evolving these guidelines to keep up with the fast-changing technology.

During his XR speaker event at XReality Pro,[26] Chris discussed how technology can assist individuals with low vision in navigating their environment. He highlighted the use of spatial audio guides to improve navigation, mobility, social interaction, communication, and assistance in daily tasks. Additionally, he emphasized the role of haptic feedback in tactile navigation and orientation, enhancing learning, education, interaction with digital content, accessible gaming, and entertainment. Moreover, Chris mentioned the use of Robot Sighted Guides for aiding people with low vision in detecting and avoiding obstacles, and in supporting education and employment opportunities.

[25] Web Content Accessibility Guidelines (WCAG), defines how to make Web content more accessible to people with disabilities. Accessibility involves a wide range of disabilities, including visual, auditory, physical, speech, cognitive, language, learning, and neurological disabilities., https://www.w3.org/TR/WCAG21, accessed Jan. 2024.
[26] XReality Pro, https://xrealitypro.com/, accessed Jan. 2024.

Microwave
Front Door
Freezer
Cooktop
Refrigerator
Oven
Sink
Island

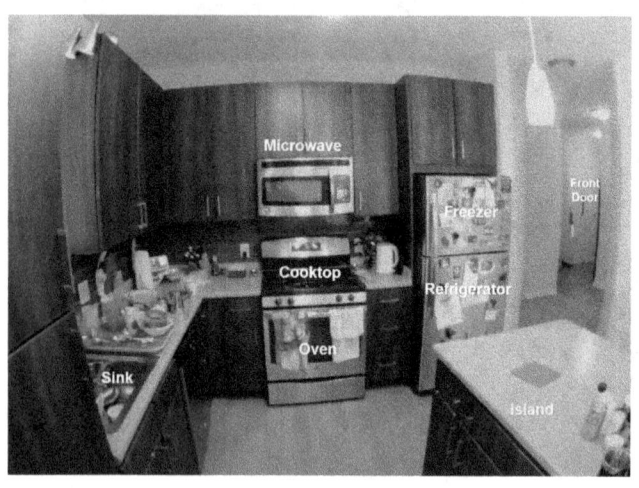

Fig. 3.16: Chris use AI and mixed reality to recognize the objects in the environment (Source: Chris McNally)

To help people with low vision, he is interested in leveraging the integration of autonomous technologies such as self-driving cars and humanoid robots, and advanced communication systems including 5G, 6G, and StarLink. These advancements are tailored to enhance accessibility and interaction for people with low vision, enabling more effective navigation and a deeper connection with their environment.

Lorelle VanFossen, director of educators in VR, highlighted the effectiveness of the Dyslexie Font[27] inside immersive spatial space, created by Dutch graphic designer Christian Boer, in aiding a dyslexic individual's reading ability. She noted that many individuals with dyslexia experience improved reading with the use of dyslexia-friendly fonts in VR spaces, proving to be an effective solution.

The PlayStation VR game *The Persistence*[28] includes carefully designed features for players with hearing impairments. Activating the hearing impairment option introduces a skull icon that shows the direction of enemies. This visual cue is only

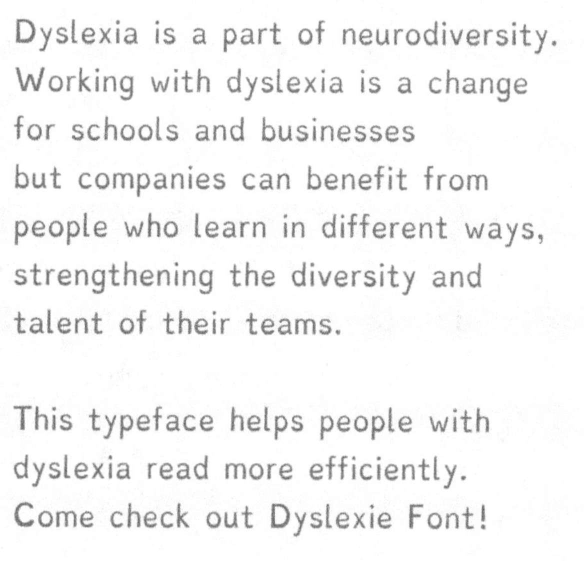

Dyslexia is a part of neurodiversity.
Working with dyslexia is a change
for schools and businesses
but companies can benefit from
people who learn in different ways,
strengthening the diversity and
talent of their teams.
This typeface helps people with
dyslexia read more efficiently.
Come check out Dyslexie Font!

Fig. 3.17: People with Dyslexia read better when using Dyslexie Font in VR space. (Reference: dyslexiefont.com)

27 Dyslexiefont.com, https://www.dyslexiefont.com, accessed Jan. 2024.
28 The Persistence, https://www.playstation.com/en-us/games/the-persistence, accessed Jan. 2024

activated in response to enemy noises, thus alerting hearing-impaired players to their proximity.

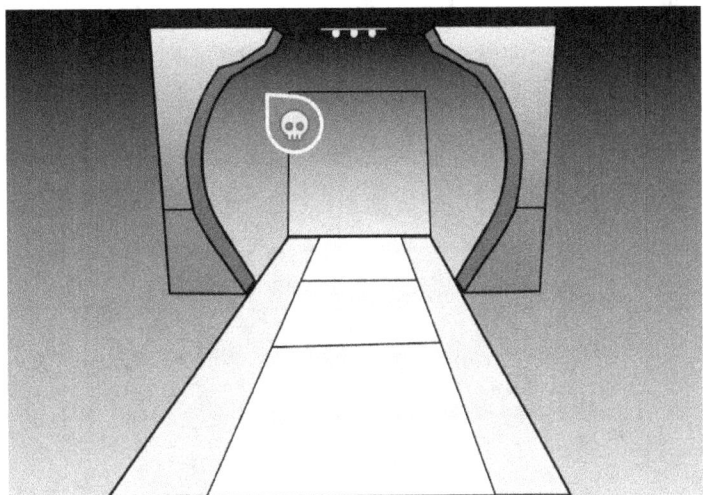

Fig. 3.18: When the hearing disability feature is activated, a skull icon appears, indicating the direction of enemies. (Source: PlayStation VR)

Moss[29] is a VR game where players assist Quill, a charming mouse, on a quest to rescue her uncle from peril. In addition to offering subtitle options for accessibility, Quill endears herself to players by using American Sign Language (ASL) for communication, especially when providing puzzle hints and emotional response, enhancing the experience for deaf players.

Permanent, Temporary, and Situational Disability

"What separates a good product from a great product is accessibility."
—Cecilia Uhr, Co-Founder of Bezi

In the Microsoft Inclusive Toolkit,[30] it is stated that everyone may experience temporary, situational, or permanent loss of certain abilities. The Toolkit emphasizes that by designing for individuals with permanent disabilities, those with situational limitations can also benefit. For instance, a device created for a person with one arm can be

---

[29] Polyarc, https://www.polyarcgames.com/games/moss, accessed Jan. 2024
[30] Microsoft Inclusive Design, https://inclusive.microsoft.design, accessed Jan. 2024.

67

equally effective for someone with a temporary wrist injury or a new parent holding an infant. This concept is referred to as the *Persona Spectrum* - when designers create with constraints in mind, they open possibilities to benefit more users than they might have originally imagined. The persona spectrum helps designers realize this by outlining constraints.[31]

---

[31] Uxbooth, https://uxbooth.com/articles/persona-spectrums-building-for-inclusion-and-accessibility, accessed Jan. 2024.

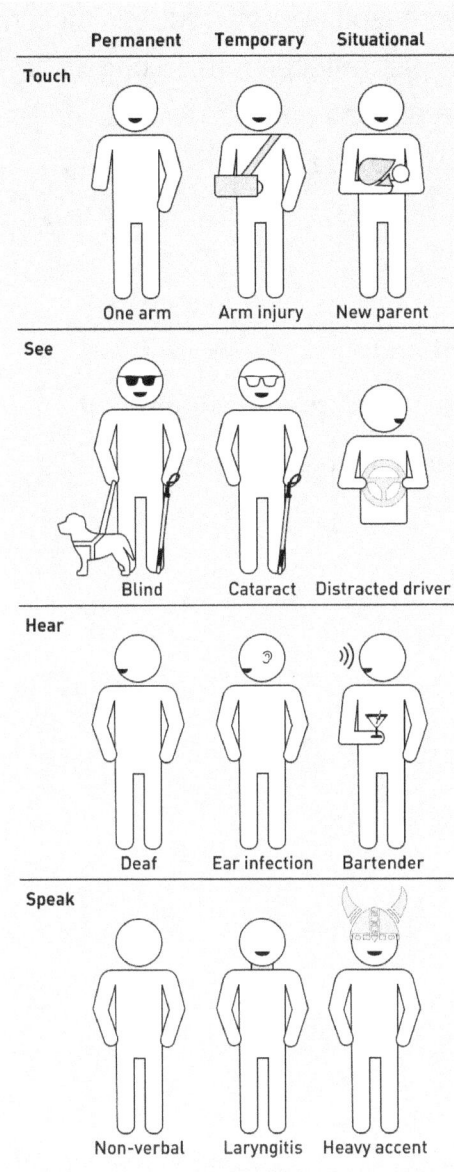

	Permanent	Temporary	Situational
Touch	One arm	Arm injury	New parent
See	Blind	Cataract	Distracted driver
Hear	Deaf	Ear infection	Bartender
Speak	Non-verbal	Laryngitis	Heavy accent

Fig. 3.19: Persona Spectrum: by designing for individuals with permanent disabilities, those with situational limitations can also benefit. (Source: Microsoft Inclusive Toolkit)

Accessibility in Spatial Design

Resources:

There are a lot of websites and organizations that help with accessibility designs. Here are a few examples:

1. **XR Access:** A community committed to making virtual, augmented, and mixed reality (XR) accessible to people with disabilities.[32]

2. **XR Accessibility User Requirements:** This document provides a comprehensive guide to the user needs and requirements for people with disabilities in virtual, augmented, or mixed reality environments. Key challenges include the overemphasis on motion controls, the need for varied input mechanisms, and audio design considerations. It emphasizes the importance of considering auditory, cognitive, neurological, physical, speech, and visual disabilities in XR design. Various input and output modalities like speech, keyboard, switch, gesture, eye tracking, tactile, visual, auditory, olfactory, and gustatory are discussed. The guide emphasizes the difficulties associated with XR controllers and underscores the necessity of customizing control inputs for compatibility across different platforms.[33] [34]

---

[32] XR Access, https://xraccess.org, accessed Jan. 2024

[33] XR Accessibility User Requirements, https://www.w3.org/TR/xaur, accessed Jan. 2024

[34] XRAccessibility, https://github.com/XRAccessibility/xraccessibility.github.io, Jan.2024

Microsoft Inclusive Design: Create technology that increases access, reduces friction, and adds emotional context for as many people as possible, reflecting these principles in their product experiences. The site also features case studies and videos that showcase how Inclusive Design is implemented in real-world scenarios.[35]

Diverse Representation

The Climb[36] is a VR game that simulates the excitement and thrill of rock climbing, offering players the chance to scale heights and explore stunning environments. It allows the player to pick the hands of different genders and skin tones to represent them.

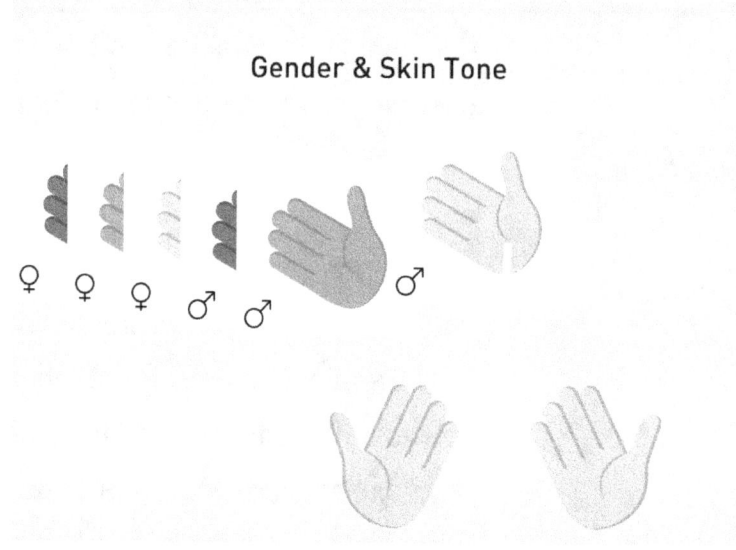

Fig. 3.20: *The Climb* is a VR game that allows the player to pick the hands of different genders and skin tones to represent them.

Rec Room is a dynamic virtual space where individuals can engage in games, craft content, and interact with others. It promotes inclusivity through extensive avatar customization options that represent a wide array of races, genders, and abilities. Meanwhile, Mozilla Hubs, an open-source initiative, empowers users to design their own VR spaces. Its browser-based accessibility ensures it is inclusive for those without advanced VR equipment. Supernatural is another inclusive VR application; this fitness

---

[35] Microsoft Inclusive Design, https://inclusive.microsoft.design, accessed Jan. 2024

[36] The Climb, https://www.theclimbgame.com, accessed Feb. 2024.

app features coaches from a multitude of backgrounds, fostering wellness and engagement in diverse communities.

Empower Women in Spatial Design

A 2021 study conducted by Accenture and Girls Who Code revealed a concerning trend in the tech industry: the proportion of women in tech roles *has decreased from 35% in 1984 to 32% in recent years.* Furthermore, the study found that half of the women who embark on a career in technology leave the field by the age of 35.[37] Companies benefit economically from gender-diverse teams, which tend to be more successful and profitable. Women's participation in spatial design also enhances user experience design and ensures that ethical and societal considerations are integrated into technology development, leading to more responsible and inclusive outcomes. This holistic approach to including women in spatial design is not only a social imperative but also a strategic business decision, essential for creating technologies that are universally beneficial and accessible.

Fostering women's involvement in spatial design involves educational support, community networks, and promoting inclusivity. Scholarships and mentorships, supportive networks, and events showcasing women's achievements in spatial design are key. It's vital to champion women in leadership, ensure equitable hiring and compensation, and facilitate resources for women-led projects. Women's active participation in development ensures diverse content, and global collaborations enhance opportunities and viewpoints for women in this cutting-edge domain.

Julie Smithson, Co-Founder of METAVERSE, emphasized the importance of diversity in all organizations, highlighting the crucial role women play in spearheading successful transformations. She pointed out that women often bring unique skills essential for detailed and innovative tasks. As leaders in any company, regardless of gender,

---

[37] AWE Blog, WOMEN'S HISTORY MONTH: CELEBRATING WOMEN IN XR, https://www.awexr.com/blog/474-women-s-history-month-celebrating-women-in-xr, accessed Jan 2024.

promoting and supporting the inclusion of more women in leadership roles is imperative. This should extend to roles that involve managing transformation processes and handling complex details. Encouraging women to venture into fields like XR and other cutting-edge sectors is essential. By creating a diverse workplace where women are encouraged to innovate, including in XR applications, companies can tap into a wider array of perspectives and skills, resulting in more effective, inventive solutions.

Karen Stritzinger believes that individuals with mentoring skills should proactively support and uplift members of underrepresented groups. Such guidance is critical for their development and success. She also feels it's vital for companies to have diverse founders and board members, instead of treating DEI as an afterthought or nice-to-have. In her experience, the initial demographic makeup of teams is often self-reinforcing and becomes harder and harder to change as time passes. Presently, less than 3% of venture capital goes to women-led ventures.[38] Successful entrepreneurs can change this by reinvesting their profits into often-neglected communities. Arlan Hamilton's endeavors serve as a key example of this strategy. Worker-owned cooperatives are also gaining traction as a model for creating more diverse and inclusive businesses. These cooperatives operate on democratic principles and equitable compensation systems, promoting fairer salary distribution among all employees.

Rahel Demant, Co-Founder of XR Bootcamp, emphasized the importance of empowering women in technology. She suggested that offering scholarships to women and supporting underrepresented talents, along with hiring more women, are crucial steps towards achieving this goal.

Amy LaMeyer emphasizes that to effectively support and empower women in the XR industry, a combination of educational opportunities, platforms for visibility, community support, and financial backing is crucial. Providing tailored teaching and training in XR

---

[38] Harvard Business Review, https://hbr.org/2023/02/for-female-founders-only-fundraising-from-female-vcs-comes-at-a-cost, accessed Jan. 2024

technologies equips women with essential skills. Amplifying their voices through interviews and conferences inspires and raises awareness. Building robust support networks offers mentorship and shared experiences. Finally, offering funding, such as grants or investments in women led XR projects, addresses financial barriers, and fosters innovation and leadership among women in the field.

Building Blocks for Diversity

Components:	Actions:
Diverse Representation	• Design avatars, environments, and narratives that represent a wide range of cultures, identities, and abilities.
Addressed (DEI) for All Spatial Design Development	• Include more gender and race diversities to be involved in the development.
Equitable Access	• Ensure the technology is accessible to users with different abilities and socioeconomic backgrounds.
Empower Women in Spatial Design	• Educational support, community networks, and promoting inclusivity. • Scholarships and mentorships, women in leadership, ensure equitable hiring and compensation, and facilitate resources for women-led projects.
Inclusive Interaction	• Develop guidelines and moderation tools to foster respectful and inclusive interactions among users.

Context

"Without context, words and actions have no meaning at all."
–Gregory Bateson

Key Design Patterns:

1. **Skeuomorphism:** Enhance user experience by leveraging familiar real-world cues, making virtual environments intuitive and immersive.[39]

2. **Realistic Virtual Objects:** By analyzing the real-world environment, the user can engage with the virtual objects through realistic lighting and shadowing.

3. **Interactivity and Engagement:** Design interactive elements that are engaging and contextually relevant. The experience should respond to user actions and environmental factors, offering a dynamic and adaptive experience.

4. **3D Objects Replace 2D Design:** Interacting with 3D objects (NUI) through hand gestures should take precedence over traditional controller-based 2D UI (GUI) manipulations.

5. **Use of Sensors and Data:** Leverage device sensors and data analytics to understand user behavior and environmental context. This can help in personalizing experiences and making them more responsive.

6. **AI Assistant:** AI assistants speak according to the context of the situation and provide help support.

---

[39] Skeuomorphism is a term most often used in graphical user interface design to describe interface objects that mimic their real-world counterparts in how they appear and/or how the user can interact with them. A well-known example is the recycle bin icon used for discarding files. Skeuomorphism makes interface objects familiar to users by using concepts they recognize. (Resource: Interaction Design Foundation, https://www.interaction-design.org/literature/topics/skeuomorphism, accessed Jan. 2024)

Why is Context Important?

Context is vital in spatial design for enhancing user experience, integrating virtual elements with the real world, ensuring safety and accessibility, and maintaining content relevance. It enables developers to create immersive, personalized experiences that adapt to different environments and user behaviors. Additionally, understanding context is key for solving specific problems efficiently, particularly in sectors like healthcare, education, and other areas where ethical considerations like privacy and cultural sensitivity are important. In essence, context shapes how spatial design technologies are experienced, ensuring they are relevant, engaging, and appropriate for their intended use. Experiencing the appropriate context is crucial for making well-informed design decisions.

What is Context?

In spatial design, context in user experience encompasses the physical environment where the experience occurs, the user's situational needs and tasks, technical limitations of the device, the user's physical and cognitive state, cultural and social factors, data privacy concerns, and the user's prior experiences with technology. Understanding these aspects is essential for creating immersive, intuitive, and safe applications that are tailored to the user's specific environment and needs, ensuring an engaging and satisfying experience.

Skeuomorphism in Contextual Design

Familiarity

Skeuomorphism is pivotal in enriching UX design in spatial environments, capitalizing on the power of familiarity. This design strategy involves crafting elements that resemble their real-world analogs, offering users intuitive and recognizable interfaces. This approach is especially beneficial in spatial design contexts, where merging digital and physical realms is crucial. In spatial design, the principle of familiarity is key to crafting immersive, user-friendly experiences. It helps minimize cognitive load, allowing users to engage with familiar, everyday concepts without the need for prior learning.

In Vision Pro, the "familiarity" concept involves converting 2D iOS applications (users already familiar with) into a 3D environment, achieved by integrating familiar elements within a seamless and immersive glass material window that seamlessly blends with the surroundings.

Fig. 3.21: Image Reference: Apple. The iOS app shares the same elements with Vision Pro UI: Sidebars, Tabs, and Search Fields. (Left is iOS, right is Vision Pro)

Use Depth to Communicate Hierarchy

Visual cues such as distance, occlusion, and shadows to grasp depth and understand their environment.

Fig. 3.22: Add shadow as the visual cue for distance.

Mirroring the Real World

"Ultrawings"[40] is another example of intuitive design, reflecting a virtual environment that closely aligns with the physical world's orientation and consistent interaction patterns. As a flight simulation game, Ultrawings VR employs Mirror Virtual Environment (MVE) technology to craft an authentic piloting experience. The game maintains a natural orientation and offers interaction patterns through intuitive controls that replicate the functionality of actual aircraft.

This allows players to seamlessly adjust to the principles of flight, enjoying a variety of aircraft and vibrant environments that feature changing weather conditions and diverse terrains. The integration of MVE with meticulous interaction design affords a deeply immersive and true-to-life virtual flight experience. The advantage of this mirroring approach is the elimination of the need for additional UI panels to instruct the user on the subsequent steps. Users can rely on their ingrained responses homed in the

---

[40] Ultrawings, https://www.meta.com/experiences/1798409083604479, accessed Feb. 2024.

physical world, thereby streamlining the learning process, and making the application more user-friendly.

Virtual Training Simulations

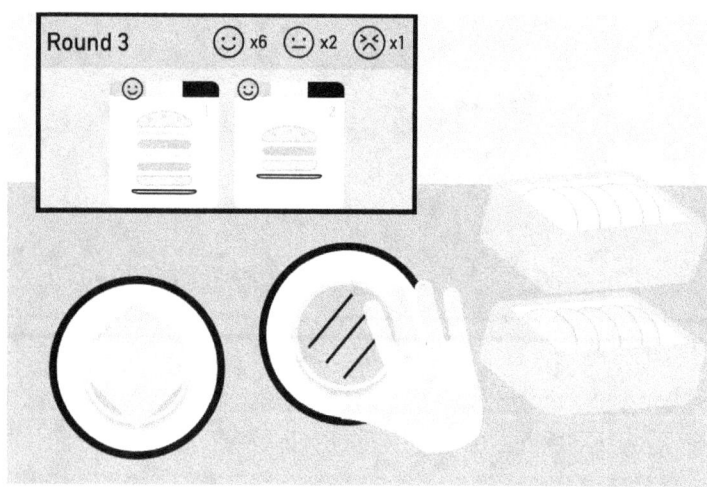

Fig. 3.23: Clash of Chefs using immersive training for food makers.

Clash of Chefs VR is a virtual reality game that immerses players in the culinary world, featuring four different cuisines: American, Italian, Japanese, and Mexican. Players are tasked with preparing and serving dishes in a bustling restaurant environment, with gameplay centering around food order management and increasing complexity. The game offers themed restaurants and tutorial videos for beginners but faces challenges with item recognition and manipulation at advanced levels. Designed with logical kitchen layouts and extensive content across twenty levels per cuisine style, it also includes a competitive multiplayer mode for a social and challenging experience.

All Virtual Objects Should Be Interactable

Lee Vermeulen underlined the crucial element of interactivity for an immersive and engaging virtual reality experience. According to him, every object in a virtual environment should be interactive, mirroring the tangible reality we experience. He also stressed the necessity of continuous playtesting, particularly for multiplayer VR games, to refine and perfect the user experience. Lee pointed out that initiating development with a prototype is more beneficial than adhering to a rigidly preconceived plan. He emphasized that VR game design is more akin to creating traditional games than to designing conventional web interfaces, highlighting the unique considerations and creative approaches required in virtual reality.

Natural User Interface (NUI)

In the realm of XR and spatial design, interactions are evolving beyond controllers towards more natural forms such as hand gestures, eye-tracking, and voice commands. Apple Vision Pro is a good example of shifting from traditional controllers to eye-hand coordination and voice activation. This device allows users to employ their gaze as a pointer, navigating the interface effortlessly, using hand gestures to select or 'click' on items.

The Vision Pro headset contains highly accurate light-sensing precision and accommodates eyeglass wearers by offering custom lens personalization based on their optical prescriptions, allowing the users to remove their glasses and fully immerse in the experience. Furthermore, the Apple Vision Pro uses Optical ID for user recognition and enhances visual accessibility for those with low vision by adjusting light contrasts, making visuals crisper and more distinct.

As for Meta Quest 3, this device brands itself as a mixed-reality headset, which has significant improvements in its passthrough capabilities from its previous headset, the Quest 2. Meta's Chief Technology Officer shared a hint of the company's prototype AR glasses as "the most sophisticated creation our species has ever engineered," indicating a future where interaction friction is minimized. This progression signifies a step towards a world where technology interfaces seamlessly with human instinct and perception.

3D Objects instead of 2D Interface

As we transition from flat, 2D experiences to immersive 3D environments, there's a growing need to rethink interface design to be more natural and intuitive. Interacting with 3D objects through hand gestures should take precedence over traditional

Fig. 3.24: Use 3D object to replace 2D UI (Grab a tangible 3D object instead of pointing at it or tap a button)

controller-based 2D UI manipulations. In a 3D space, elements should exist within the environment, offering tangible qualities such as temperature, texture, and depth—qualities that a simple 2D interface lacks. The physicality of even a single sheet of paper, with its distinct feel and ability to be manipulated in space, demonstrates the potential for more engaging interactions. By leveraging the full potential of immersive spaces for storytelling and interaction, designers can create experiences that feel organic and are truly at one with their surroundings.

Pillow weaves storytelling into an immersive space, transforming the gaming experience by replacing traditional 2D interfaces with interactive 3D objects. Selection within the game is intuitive and tactile; players reach out to grasp and manipulate 3D objects directly, moving away from the conventional method of clicking 2D buttons.

Onboarding & Tutorials in Contextual Design

"Train by doing, instead of describing what to do, avoid information overload to create a meaningful experience."
–Kyle Morrand

Onboarding and tutorials are designed to help users grasp the context-specific interactions within the app, particularly targeting newcomers or those unfamiliar with the technology. These tools impart crucial knowledge about the app's context, including operation, control, and the why and how of usage. In spatial design, it's essential to make these elements intuitive. Tutorials serve as an essential bridge, acquainting users, and players with the knowledge they need before jumping into an immersive environment. The reliance on tutorials points to a gap in intuitiveness; the virtual and spatial realms haven't seamlessly aligned with real-world interactions; it still needs guidance on using controllers and interfaces.

Lorelle VanFossen, Director of Educators in VR, emphasizes that textual information is generally overlooked in VR environments. Her advice is to demonstrate rather than tell: if you have a story, visualize it. Extensive text instructions on a UI panel are likely to be ignored, underscoring the importance of show over tell in VR experiences. Here are some common ways to create tutorials to efficiently guide the users:

1. **Guided Tutorials:** Offer interactive tutorials that guide users through the basic controls and functionalities of the spatial design environment, ensuring they feel comfortable and prepared. For example, Meta Horizon Worlds provides a dedicated tutorial space for first-time players, complete with controller training. This includes visual UI instructions and a simulated environment where users can practice navigation and adjust movement settings, transitioning between "Slide" and "Teleportation" locomotion.

Fig. 3.25: A specialized tutorial area tailored for newcomers, offering comprehensive controller training to ease players into the experience.

HoloNotes in ShapesXR is an innovative feature allowing users to record and place avatar movements as spatial comments in virtual environments. Users can easily create a Holonote by recording their avatar, adjusting the viewpoint, and adding comments. These notes can be played, managed, and removed through various intuitive controls. With options for visibility toggling and a maximum duration of two minutes per note, Holonotes enhances asynchronous design reviews by focusing on spatial elements and improving team communication in virtual spaces.

Fig. 3.26: HoloNotes, a feature within ShapesXR, enables users to capture and embed their avatar movements as spatial annotations within virtual settings. (Source: ShapesXR)

2. **Intuitive Hint:** Employ clear, concise language and recognizable visuals, sounds, haptics to guide users. Make sure the interaction techniques, whether they involve gestures or controller inputs, are instinctive and maintain uniformity across the entire application. For instance, the Gorilla Tag VR game, which utilizes a charcoal-styled arrow to signify the motion of arm swinging required for movement within the game. This approach offers a straightforward method for acclimating new players.

Fig. 3.27: In the Gorilla Tag VR game, it uses arrows to indicate arms swinging motions to guide players on how to move within the game, providing a straightforward and intuitive way to introduce new players to the controls. (Source: Gorilla Tag VR)

3. **Contextual Assistance:** Provide contextual help or tips when users seem to struggle with a specific feature or task. This can be detected through their actions or the amount of time they spend on a particular task.

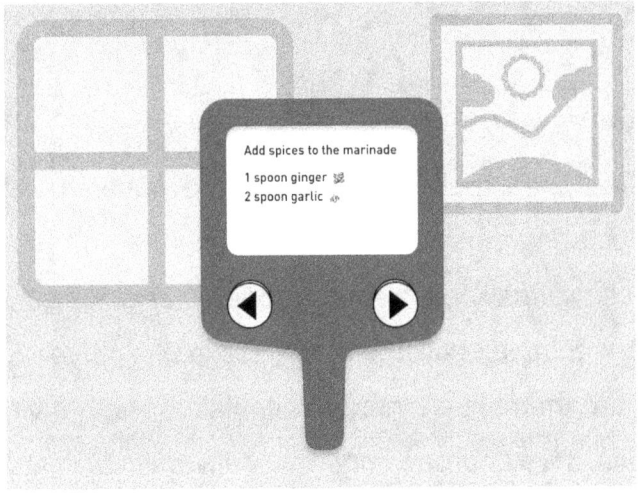

Fig. 3.28: It employs engaging, step-by-step instructions to guide users in rediscovering lost recipes. (Source: Lost Recipe)

4. **Progressive Onboarding:** Introduce features progressively to avoid overwhelming new users. Start with basic functionalities and gradually expose more complex features as they get more comfortable. For example, *Pillow* employs a progressive interactive approach to onboarding. Players can choose from a selection of experiences, each with a unique story and interaction style.

Before each story begins, an introductory video provides context for the upcoming experience.

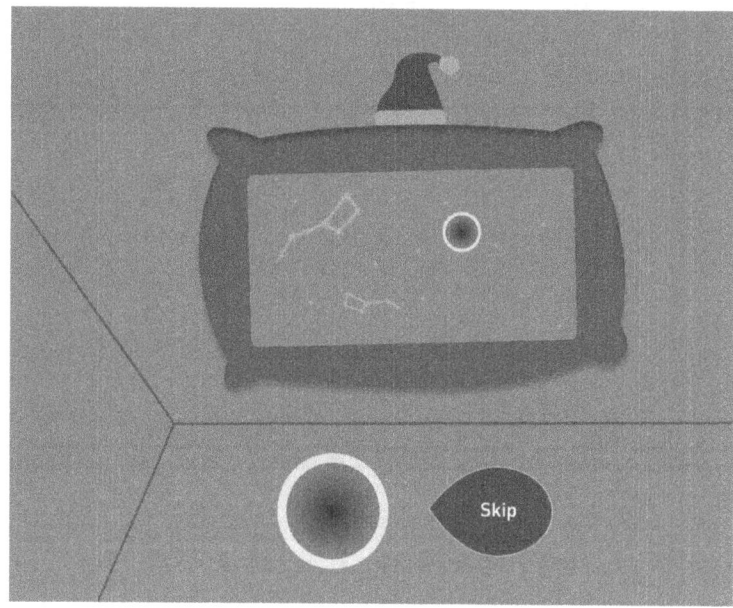

Fig. 3.29: Players can choose from a selection of experiences, each with a unique story and interaction style. Before each story begins, an introductory video provides context for the upcoming experience. (Source: Pillow)

5. **Quick Wins:** Craft the experience to ensure new users quickly attain a sense of achievement, fostering motivation to further explore. In LEGO® Bricktales, the game introduces gradually escalating tutorials, ranging from basic controller handling to more complex building block usage. As players progress, they create structures that are then tested through simulations with a virtual robot navigating the constructions. This approach not only delivers incremental victories but also sets clear, specific goals to meet, enhancing user engagement and learning.

Fig. 3.30: In LEGO® Bricktales, it creates quick wins to help users learn and onboard. (Source: LEGO® Bricktales)

6. **Playful Intuitive Learning:** Use a "Playful" way to intuitively teach the users how to interact. *First Steps for Quest 2* offers a selection of interactive materials that guide the player through hands-on learning experiences. These materials are designed to teach the player how to effectively use controllers through engaging gameplay.

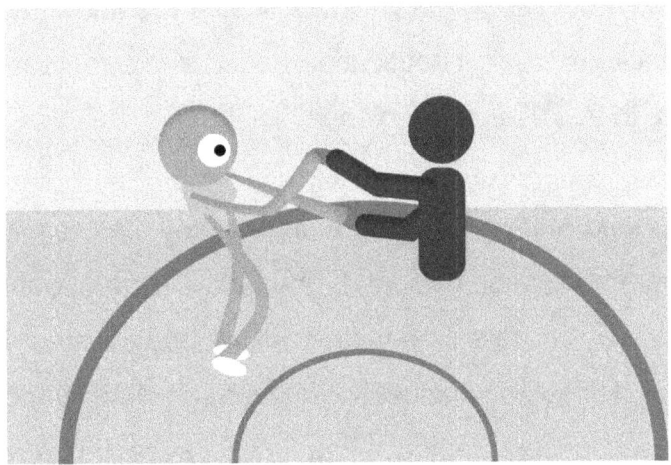

Fig. 3.31: First Steps for Quest 2, dance with a robot. (Source: Meta)

In spatial design settings, where physical and virtual realities intertwine, aim for clarity, and minimize cognitive load through Skeuomorphism and Natural User Interfaces (NUI) rather than Graphical User Interfaces (GUI). Use 3D objects over traditional 2D flat screens and incorporate effective onboarding and tutorials.

AI Assistant - Digital Assistant

"70% of human communication is non-verbal. We can't ignore the fact that visual communication is just as important as voice communication."
-David Colleen

AI digital assistant, also known as a virtual assistant or mobile assistant, is a technology designed to assist users by answering questions and handling simple tasks. These assistants aim to save users time on routine activities that do not require human intervention. AI assistants can provide support through voice commands, and interactions will be naturally initiated by gestures, gaze, and speech. In this smarter, more intuitive setting, iris scanning allows the computer to understand users' needs, emotions, and health situations to create a seamless experience, potentially rendering tutorials obsolete. Familiar examples include voice-activated assistants like Siri and Alexa, which respond to everyday commands. In the digital workplace, digital assistants help employees find information and process tasks such as approvals and service desk tickets. They can be customized for businesses of all sizes and offer more than just conversational interfaces, including notification-based and app-based interactions, known as microapps, to suit user convenience.

SapientX offers advanced AI technology with several key features. Their approach emphasizes visual communication through high-quality avatars, enhancing user interaction and trust. They utilize data mining from various sources, for accurate information retrieval. Their system includes sentiment analysis, understanding user emotions for tailored responses. SapientX has its own speech recognition system and offers synthetic speech that can mimic various voices. They also incorporate machine vision for object and person recognition, maintaining user privacy. Additionally, their system supports multiple languages, automatically adapting to the user's language choice.

Building Blocks for Context

Components:	Actions:
Skeuomorphism	• leveraging familiar real-world cues, making virtual environments intuitive and immersive.
3D Objects NUI Interaction to Replace 2D GUI	• Understanding the user's context, provide information and interactions
All Virtual Objects Should Be Interactable	• Every object in a virtual environment should be interactive, mirroring the tangible reality we experience.
Guided Tutorials	• Offer interactive tutorials that guide users through the basic training of the spatial design environment.
Intuitive Hint	• Employ clear, concise language and recognizable visuals, sounds, and haptics to guide users.
Contextual Assistance	• Provide contextual help or tips when users seem to struggle with a specific feature or task.
Progressive Onboarding	• Introduce features progressively to avoid overwhelming new users.
Quick Wins	• Craft the experience to ensure new users quickly attain a sense of achievement, fostering motivation to further explore.
Playful Intuitive Learning	• Incorporate playful methods to intuitively guide users in learning interactions.

Connect

"We are all connected; to each other, biologically; to the earth, chemically; to the rest of the universe atomically."
—Neil deGrasse Tyson

Key Strategies

1. **Enhancing User Engagement and Immersion:** Connection Between Virtual and Physical World. Elevating the overall experience to be more captivating and unforgettable.

2. **Connect Across Different Devices:** Look for tools that allow for different immersive experiences across different devices (e.g., WebXR).

3. **Blend the Virtual and Physical Space:** Enables users to interact with their environment, including IoT and spatial computing, through natural user interfaces (NUI) like voice, eye movements, and hand gestures. This integration blurs the lines between virtual and physical spaces, transforming IoT into a seamless blend of virtual and physical domains.

4. **Personalization and Contextual Relevance:** By understanding the user's context, spatial computing applications can provide information and interactions that are directly relevant to the user's current situation or environment.

5. **Collaboration and Social Interaction:** By connecting users across different physical locations, these technologies break down geographical barriers and enable collaborative experiences that were previously not possible.

6. **Connect Different Industries:** In education and training, XR and spatial computing enhances learning by making complex concepts tangible, interactive, and engaging. In healthcare, XR innovatively connects patients with treatments, like using virtual worlds for effective pain management. Additionally, XR allows

brands to create unique, immersive experiences that deeply resonate with their audiences, offering a novel way of interaction and engagement.

Why is Connect Important?

Fig. 3.32: Imran Chaudhri, CEO of Humane, said on Ted Talk "The future is not in your face". We don't want our kids living in an isolated virtual world.

In the early days, VR was a solitary experience, confining users within their headsets and isolating them during gameplay. The immersive environment was personal and invisible to onlookers, as Humane's[41] CEO Imran Chaudhri reflected in his TED Talk,[42] hinting at a future beyond head-mounted displays. While VR unlocked new realms of creativity and experience, it also pushed us away from real-world connections. While Humane may address "Connection" issues by eliminating headsets, it risks compromising privacy by not offering a visual presentation of sensitive information.

The depth of visual display could be a crucial element for an additional layer of connection. In a Humane demo, when a user asked about a gate code, Humane read the gate code aloud. John Hanacek raised concerns over the security implications of such voice-activated responses for confidential queries. He stressed the risk associated with sole reliance on auditory feedback, particularly in contexts demanding high privacy.

---

[41] Humane AI Pin - the device is designed to be screenless and operates independently, focusing on privacy and natural interaction without the need for a wake word or constant listening. The Ai Pin includes AI-powered features and a laser-projected display, aiming to redefine personal mobile computing in the AI era. The company promotes a future where technology provides a human-centric, intuitive experience built on trust and privacy.

[42] Imran Chaudhri CEO of Humane, The Disappearing Computer — and a World Where You Can Take AI Everywhere", https://www.youtube.com/watch?v=gMsQO5u7-NQ, accessed Jan, 2024

In environments where revealing personal information like banking details, medical records, or passwords is perilous, spoken responses could breach privacy. John advocated for visually displaying sensitive information as a more secure option, rather than announcing it vocally. This approach not only enhances user privacy but also extends Humane's functionality, introducing subtler and more flexible interaction possibilities.

Additionally, research by Potter MC, Wyble B, and Hagmann CE emphasized the brain's reliance on visual information "90 percent of information transmitted to the brain is visual,"[43] and David Colleen pointed out that most human communication is non-verbal. Compared with AI Pin, spatial computing and XR have the visual presentation aspect which will have more options for presenting the data.

Spatial computing is moving towards a future where technology like XREAL and Ray-Ban's sleek designs enable social connection and co-presence, mitigating digital isolation and fostering a more connected human experience. A demonstration showcases Meta's vision of AR glasses enabling a user to engage and play chess with a holographic avatar in real-life. This can create a true sense of connection.

---

[43] Potter MC, Wyble B, Hagmann CE, McCourt ES. Detecting meaning in RSVP at 13 ms per picture. *Atten Percept Psychophys.* 2014;76:270. doi: 10.3758/s13414-013-0605-z. [PubMed] [CrossRef] [Google Scholar]

Fig. 3.33: A demonstration showcases Meta's vision of AR glasses enabling individuals to engage in holographic chess gameplay. (Concept: Meta)

What is Connect?

Connect has two essential meanings: To join two things, or to be joined together, and to create a relationship between two or more people, groups, or things. In the realm of spatial computing, we can distill the core benefits into three interconnected categories:

1. **Bridging the Virtual and Physical Worlds:** This category encompasses the integration of digital elements with the physical environment, allowing for a seamless flow between the two realms.

2. **Fostering Collaboration and Social Interaction:** Here, the focus is on using spatial computing to enhance cooperative efforts and social connections, regardless of the physical distance between individuals or groups.

Bridging the Virtual and Physical Worlds

1. **Connection Between Virtual and Physical World:**

   The Vision Pro "EyeSight" aims to enhance the perception of those around the headset wearer. Despite the wearer's eyes being covered by the headset, the external display shows a recorded view of the wearer's eyes to create the illusion that they are looking through the device. Apple has included a tutorial in the beta, termed "Persona Enrollment," to guide users through the process of setting up face and eye recording for the external display. Setup involves the user holding the headset with its forward-facing cameras and prompts from Vision Pro instruct the user to look in different directions, similar in principle to the initial configuration of Face ID. This feature adds a layer of interactivity and personalization to the user's digital representation in the Vision Pro experience.

Fig. 3.34: EyeSight: The external display on Apple Vision Pro reveals your eyes, signaling when you're engaged with apps or fully immersed, providing visibility to those around you.

2. **Enable Seamless Immersive Experiences Across Platforms:**

   WebXR enables cross-platform immersive experiences primarily due to its web-based framework, which ensures universal compatibility across various devices and browsers. It abstracts hardware complexities, offering a unified interface for diverse XR and spatial computing inputs, and eliminates the need for device-specific software, allowing users to access experiences directly through a web browser. This approach, combined with its integration with standard web technologies and ongoing standardization by the World Wide Web Consortium (W3C), makes WebXR a versatile tool for creating accessible, wide-reaching immersive environments.

Ben Erwin, creator at The Poly Awards, is for an immersive and open Metaverse. He agrees with the concept of seamless digital asset transfer across platforms, mirroring the fluidity of web hyperlinks, and stresses the need for uniform interaction standards across diverse interfaces like desktops and touchscreens, recognizing the potential of emerging technologies. For WebXR to have a smooth experience across different devices and browsers, it requires a unified input system across different devices and browsers.

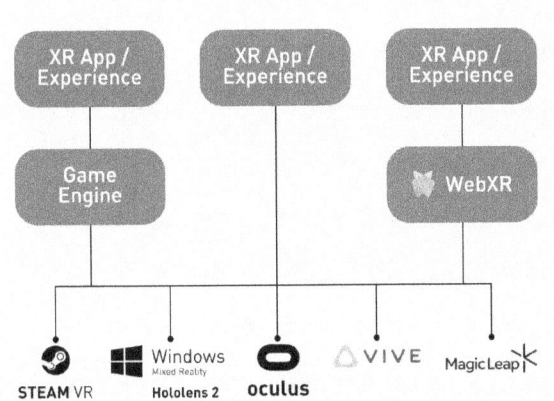

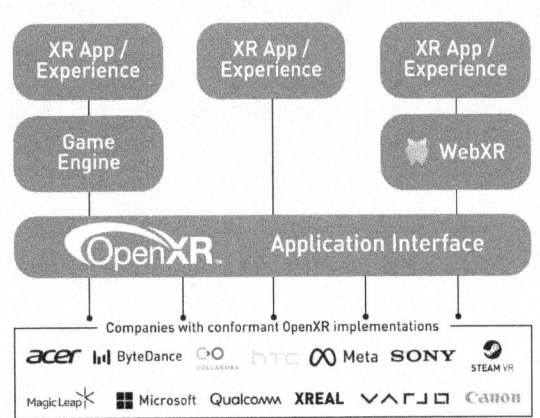

Fig. 3.35: Without a universal standard, VR and AR apps must rely on platform-specific APIs, and new input devices require tailored drivers.

Fig. 3.36: OpenXR offers a unified path into device environments on multiple platforms. It allows applications and engines, such as WebXR, to operate on any system that implements the OpenXR interfaces.

3. **Connect and Interact with the Data Painted on the World:**

In the book *Convergence*,[44] Charlie Fink, Columnist at Forbes, mentioned that *"The world will be painted with Data"* in 2019. AR and spatial computing are increasingly integrated into various aspects of daily life. Navigation is simplified with AR-based directional overlays in the real-world. In retail, they enable virtual try-on experiences; in education, they enhance learning through interactive 3D visualizations. Healthcare benefits from AR in surgeries with real-time data overlay, while real estate uses it for virtual property tours. Maintenance sectors employ AR for efficient equipment repairs through interactive guides. The gaming and entertainment industries are transformed by AR's immersive experiences, and advertising leverages AR for interactive and engaging consumer campaigns. These applications showcase AR's role in bridging the digital and physical realms, enhancing both functionality and user experience across diverse fields. AR connects us through visualizations of the data painted on the world.

4. **Blend the Virtual and Physical Space:**

In the YouTube video "Spatial Computing DEMO-1 'Programmable Space'" by VRCrew,[45] the developers showcased an innovative space that responds to hand gestures. This environment, powered by a head-mounted display (HMD), features a digital twin that is in real-time, bi-directional synchronization with the physical world. The technology leverages IoT and computer vision, seamlessly integrating the virtual and real worlds. When a user, wearing the headset, can tap their fingers on a physical lamp, causing the light within the lamp to turn on. This type of interaction, previously likened to magic or superpowers, exemplifies the capabilities of spatial computing. It enables the natural user interfaces (NUI) to interact with the environment, bridging the gap between the virtual and physical realms.

---

[44] Charlie Fink and more authors, Convergence: How The World Will Be Painted With Data, June 9, 2019
[45] VRCREW, Spatial Computing DEMO-1 "Programmable Space",https://www.youtube.com/watch?v=GRuJCernS7s, accessed Jan. 2024

Fig. 3.37: In the video, the girl was able to interact with the light in the physical world through a headset by tapping her fingers. (Source: VRCREW, Spatial Computing DEMO-1 "Programmable Space")

DoublePoint[46] integrated real-world objects to provide authentic tactile feedback is crucial for enhancing virtual experiences, enabling a more natural interaction within these digital realms. It has products such as wrist-based ray casting, eye tracking, and smart IoT control, which allows the user to use hand gesture control of the physical world such as turning off the light.

Fostering Collaboration and Social Interaction

Photorealistic in Spatial Space

In Lex Fridman on of the Podcast show[47] Mark Zuckerberg and Lex Fridman discussed the advancements in photo realistic avatars, emphasizing the enhanced sense of presence and intimacy these avatars bring to virtual interactions. Zuck highlighted the potential of mixed reality experiences, where digital and physical worlds merge, especially in meetings and gaming. Fridman was notably impressed by the technology's

---

[46] DoublePoint, https://www.doublepoint.com/product, Accessed Jan. 2024.

[47] Lex Fridman, Mark Zuckerberg: First Interview in the Metaverse | Lex Fridman Podcast #398, https://www.youtube.com/watch?v=MVYrJJNdrEg, accessed Jan. 2024

ability to capture subtle expressions, particularly around the eyes, which contributed to the realism of the conversation. The interview showcased the significant progress made in virtual reality technology and its potential to transform communication and interaction in the digital realm.

Apple's Vision Pro elevates FaceTime by introducing a spatial experience where participants appear life-size, and Spatial Audio aligns voices with their virtual positions. Users on Vision Pro are represented by their "Persona," a realistic, spatial avatar displaying real-time facial expressions and hand movements. This advanced feature, created swiftly through machine learning, extends to other video conferencing platforms like Zoom, Cisco Webex, and Microsoft Teams, offering a more immersive and dynamic communication experience across various applications.

Connect in the Virtual World

In designing virtual spaces for business and prototyping, aligning with user objectives like presentations, collaboration, meetings, and private areas is essential, especially considering many users may not be familiar with gaming. Simplicity in interaction, such as intuitive hand gestures (grabbing, tapping), rather than complex controller functions, is crucial for reducing cognitive load and enhancing user-friendliness. Cross-platform compatibility, including 2D platforms for easy meeting management and file uploads, is necessary for seamless collaboration. Arkio exemplifies this by allowing 2D (PC and Mobile) and 3D virtual space users to work together, incorporating mixed reality for real-time collaboration.

Regarding game design in virtual worlds, platforms like VRChat cater to the younger generation by offering freedom in the world and avatar creation, emphasizing customized experiences. Gorilla Tag creates a unique environment by transforming players into gorillas. For such platforms, moderation and safety are vital to protect younger users.

The design approach should focus on direct, intuitive interactions, utilizing eye-hand coordination and voice commands, making it accessible for non-gaming professionals. Simplifying the virtual environment by organizing it into distinct spaces like presentation rooms, learning areas, collaboration rooms, galleries, and private spaces can enhance functionality. This approach allows for cooling down, meditating, or working alone in private spaces. UI should be straightforward, with tools accessible via controllers or hand gestures for creation and moderation. For example, ShapesXR utilizes controller UI for quick tool access, demonstrating the importance of intuitive design in virtual collaboration.

Digital Pets: Emotion Connect

Susan Cummings pointed to virtual pets as a solution for individuals who cannot have physical pets due to allergies or limited space. This concept allows people to creatively design their own digital companions without restrictions. Furthermore, she delved into the possibility of digitally preserving a pet's unique traits and personality, thereby extending its legacy to future generations. This would involve using AI to capture and replicate a pet's distinctive sounds and movements. As a result, after a pet's demise, its digital counterpart, mirroring the original's behavior and appearance, could be created. Moreover, she highlighted the potential of AI in mimicking the tone and responses of a specific individual, adding a more personalized touch to the virtual pet experience. These digital companions not only provide comfort and deep emotional connections but also represent a remarkable innovation in the digital realm.

Platforms for Business

VirBELA[48] offers a virtual campus for business collaboration, featuring spaces for meetings and offices in a virtual world. ENGAGE[49] serves as an educational and training platform, also catering to business meetings and professional development. BizzTech[50] stands out with its ability to link metaverse presence to domain names,

[48] VirBELA, https://www.virbela.com, accessed Jan. 2024.
[49] ENGAGE, https://engagevr.io, accessed Jan. 2024.
[50] Bizztech, https://bizztech.io, accessed Jan. 2024.

enhancing business control. Mozilla Hubs[51] is an open-source project for creating VR social experiences, used by businesses for custom meeting environments. Immersed focuses on individual and team productivity, enabling work in mixed reality with multiple screens in a shared space. Horizon Worlds[52] has a business section for brand awareness and different promotions creatively. It also has a creator tool that allows the creators to quickly prototype with simple code or no code.

Fig. 3.38: In BizzTech, business profession virtual world meeting. It allows 2D screen meetings and 3D avatar meetings in a highly polished professional business meeting room.

Platforms for Collaborations/Prototype

ShapesXR, Arkio,[53] and Gravity Sketch[54] are innovative mixed reality prototyping tools tailored for design and collaboration. ShapesXR facilitates collaboration among designers and experts from ideation to final creation. Arkio specializes in designing interiors, buildings, and virtual spaces, supporting multiple devices from PC to XR headsets for collaborative work. Gravity Sketch provides a virtual studio for designers to create, communicate, and share 3D designs at every step of the design process, enhancing workflow efficiency and creativity.

[51] Mozilla, https://hubs.mozilla.com, accessed Jan. 2024
[52] Horizon Worlds, https://www.meta.com/experiences/2532035600194083, accessed Jan. 2024
[53] ARKIO, https://www.arkio.is, accessed Jan. 2024.
[54] Gravity Sketch, https://www.gravitysketch.com, accessed Jan. 2024.

Spatial computing is revolutionizing various sectors by merging virtual and physical realities, thereby enhancing collaboration and integration. It bridges the gap between digital and real-world experiences, improving communication and fostering a stronger sense of presence. Lifelike avatars in this space allow for a better understanding of non-verbal cues, aiding in collaborative concept visualization. This technology plays a pivotal role in diverse applications, from virtual try-ons in retail, assisting surgeries in healthcare, to streamlining processes in manufacturing. In business, multiplayer platforms merge real and virtual environments, facilitating meaningful experiences in work, collaboration, and leisure. In education and training, XR transforms learning into a more tangible, interactive, and engaging process. In healthcare, XR, particularly VR, offers innovative patient treatment methods, such as virtual worlds for pain management. Additionally, XR enables brands to create immersive experiences that profoundly connect with their audiences.

Connect Subject Matter Experts

XR and Spatial computing can help users of different backgrounds work on sample projects from ideations to collaboration. For example, Nanome[55] is an Extended Reality (XR) platform designed to help subject matter experts like Medicinal Chemists, Computational Chemists, and Structural Biologists, as well as educators and students, visualize and collaborate in virtual space. It serves as a powerful tool for collaboration, communication, and ideation, catering specifically to the pharmaceutical and educational sectors. During COVID, scientists use Nanome to work together and figure out a cure and work on vaccines for COVID.

---

[55] Nanome, https://nanome.ai, accessed Jan. 2024.

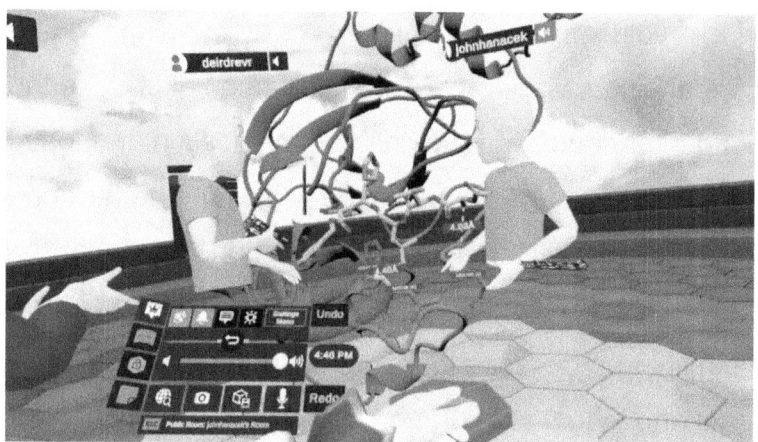

Fig. 3.39: Nanome is a collaborative tool that enables SMEs to visualize their concepts, collaborate effectively, brainstorm ideas, and present solutions in Virtual Reality (VR) and Mixed Reality (MR). (Source: Nanome)

In Nanome, subject matter experts (SMEs) can immerse themselves and visualize molecules in a manner previously unattainable. John Hanacek noted that numerous scientists were moved upon witnessing their target molecule or protein rendered as 3D structures within Nanome for the first time. After years of observing these structures in 2D on screens and in textbooks, the palpable realism of the 3D representations brought them new insights that were not obvious all the time before viewed in 2D. Nanome supports numerous molecular file types and data types including the "Electron Density Map" associated with a structure when it was captured in real life at atomic scale by X-Ray Crystallography. This type of 3D structural data is difficult if impossible to comprehend in 2D yet easily explorable in XR.

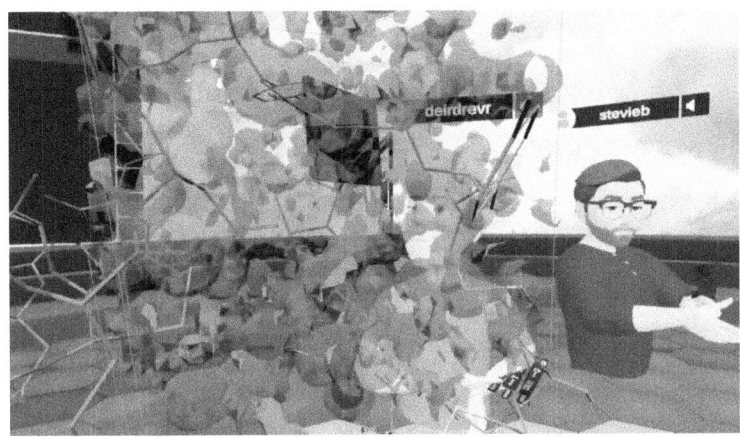

Fig. 3.40: In Nanome, "Electron Density Map" allows the scientists to view original data used to construct molecular files. (Source: Nanome)

In the dynamic field of biology, much like molecules themselves, nothing remains static. Within the realm of simulation, molecules are represented in 4D—encompassing three-dimensional space plus the dimension of time. This portrayal of molecules as wiggling entities provides scientists with a more realistic understanding of molecular behavior as it occurs in the natural world. Nanome enables scientists to interact with these molecular models by scaling them up or down, thereby enhancing their visualization capabilities. This level of manipulation facilitates easier measurements of interatomic distances, paving the way for potential modifications and innovations in molecular design.

Fig. 3.41: Molecular Dynamics simulations (jokingly called wiggling molecules) are represented in 4D—encompassing three-dimensional space plus the dimension of time as frames of the simulation playback. (Source: Nanome)

Nanome also allows the scientists to dynamically present the ideas by enabling "Grab Presenting Mode" - whoever grabs the molecule is the presenter, this allows the collaborations to become diverse and interactive, facilitating the collaboration.

Fig. 3.42: The user can shrink the molecule very small or enlarge it very big to work inside the molecule. (Source: Nanome)

Building Blocks for Connect

Components:	Actions:
Enhancing User Engagement and Immersion	• Connection Between Virtual and Physical World
Personalization and Contextual Relevance	• Understanding the user's context, provide information and interactions
WebXR	• Connect the Immersive Experience Through Different Devices
Enhanced Accessibility	• Providing individuals with disabilities unique ways to interact with their environment.
Blend the Virtual and Physical Space	• Transforming IoT into a seamless blend of virtual and physical domains.
Collaboration and Social Interaction	• Break down geographical barriers
Connect Subject Matter Experts (SMEs) From Different Backgrounds	• Bring the SMEs together in different industries such as Medical, Education, Healthcare, Retail, Collaboration, and more.

Comfort

"The role of the designer is to create space for human comfort."
- Philippe Starck

Key Design Patterns:

1. **Ergonomic Design for All Body Types:** Designing hardware and wearables that comfortably fit a diverse range of body sizes and shapes, enhancing the user experience for a broader audience.

2. **Haptic Feedback:** Provide immediate, error-preventing feedback on user actions and make XR experiences more accessible.

3. **Movement:** Arm swinging, real walking (room-scale), vehicle-based movement, or teleportation in VR.

4. **Visual Comfort:** Opt for gentle, non-flickering lighting and a soothing, cohesive color scheme, simple textures, and depth indication to avoid eye strain and discomfort.

5. **Center Important Content within the Field of View:** Make sure the important content is within the user's visual range.

6. **Dynamic Scale:** Dynamic scaling ensures that content remains easily readable and interactive, irrespective of its distance from the user.

7. **Comfortable UI Scale, Position, Timing, and Fonts:** When creating a 2D UI experience, ensure the UI's scale, timing, position, and font are tailored to the gameplay to avoid visual discomfort.

8. **Audio Comfort:** To enhance immersion in virtual environments, utilize 3D spatial audio for environmental cues and ensure ambient sounds match the setting.

9. **Shared Space - Private, Collaborate, and Present:** From individual workspaces and collaborative areas to private and public rooms, a good working space should have good designs to tailor all the needs.

10. **Scale in the Shared Space is important:** Avatar keeps the same scale only in the teleport and play mode. Otherwise, the players can change scales. It is important to make sure the scale is right, wrong scale is a bad experience in the shared space.

11. **Private and Public Space:** Make sure to keep private when the user is in a private space or not in the same virtual space. You can show a stylish 3D icon or headshot, not a full-body avatar.

Why is Comfort Important?

In spatial environments, comfort is the primary factor for design. Unlike PC gaming, where discomfort from issues like latency, choppy animation, or poor texture quality might be tolerable on a small screen, these issues become magnified in immersive environments. Imagine being in a room where everything, from the walls to the furniture, is rendered in low-resolution, bad textures. Encountering a life-sized avatar with awkward, zombie-like movements and incorrect orientation can be jarring. Additionally, a large, obtrusive UI that blocks your view and cannot be turned off exacerbates the discomfort, making you feel trapped and disoriented in a bizarre, uncontrollable space. This highlights the importance of high-quality visuals, smooth animations, and user-friendly interface design in creating comfortable and engaging spatial experiences.

What is Comfort?

Comfort entails experiencing a sense of control, freedom from pain, and a feeling of security. In spatial environments, comfort is paramount to prevent disorientation and "motion sickness," ensuring a positive user experience. Comfortable design not only fosters longer and more frequent use, enhancing engagement across gaming, training, and educational applications but also drives broader adoption, crucial for the growth of spatial computing technologies in various sectors. Additionally, ergonomic considerations in design prevent physical strain and injuries, especially in applications requiring extended use. Beyond physical health, comfortable spatial experiences are vital for mental well-being, reducing stress and promoting relaxation, thereby reinforcing their overall appeal and effectiveness.

Amy LaMeyer highlights that to ensure user comfort in spatial experiences, several key challenges must be addressed. These include the optimization of headset design for effective heat dissipation, balanced weight, and adjustable fits to accommodate glasses wearers. Stabilizing the frame rate is essential to mitigate motion sickness, alongside refining movement tracking for a seamless alignment between virtual and physical motions. Additionally, usability improvements play a crucial role, such as facilitating content downloads, long battery life, ensuring easy navigation and interaction within spaces, incorporating intuitive interaction methods like voice control, and simplifying both device connectivity and content creation. Tackling these issues can lead to a substantial improvement in the overall user experience.

Here are some ways to create comfort in spatial design:

1. **Body Comfort:** Headset, Haptic, and Motion Movement.
2. **Mind Comfort:** Visual and Audio.
3. **Soul Comfort:** Shared Space and co-presence.

Body Comfort

Ergonomic Design for All Body Types

Arwa Michelle Mboya,[56] an experienced design manager and creative director, conducted an in-person experiment in January 2020 at the MIT Media Lab. Her project,

---

[56] Arwa Michelle Mboya, Experience Design Manager & Creative Director, https://www.linkedin.com/in/arimichellemboya

Allo-I,[57] is a virtual reality human interaction study focusing on the lives and experiences of Black women, particularly those in Kenyan informal settlements in Nairobi. During her research, she discovered that the Oculus Go headset did not fit Black women comfortably due to its tight head strap, as many Black women have a significant amount of hair. To address this issue, Mboya innovatively designed a new head strap, tailored specifically for Black women, ensuring a better and more comfortable fit for the headset.

As an Asian woman with a smaller nose, I encountered fitting issues with the first generation of Ray-Ban smart glasses. They constantly slid off my face, necessitating the purchase of additional nose pads for support. The design of these glasses seemed more suited for facial structures common in white populations, characterized by a shorter nose support. This design oversight meant that I had to use extra nose pads to prevent the glasses from slipping, which hindered my enjoyment and the immersive experience offered by the first generation of Ray-Ban smart glasses. This experience highlights a broader issue where the enjoyment and immersion of wearable tech can be compromised for individuals due to designs that don't accommodate diverse facial features.

Good ergonomics in XR headsets and controllers are crucial for a comfortable and immersive experience. Key aspects include a lightweight headset design to minimize neck strain, with evenly distributed weight and adjustable straps to fit various head sizes comfortably. Adequate padding, especially around the forehead and cheeks, along with balanced weight distribution, reduces pressure on the face and nose. Proper ventilation and anti-fogging features are essential for prolonged use. The ability to adjust the interpupillary distance (IPD) ensures a clear visual experience. For controllers, an ergonomic design with easy-to-reach buttons and natural hand fit is vital, along with haptic feedback for tactile sensations and wireless capabilities to enhance freedom of movement and avoid cable entanglement. For Vision Pro, use Face ID on your iPhone

---

[57] Arwa Michelle Mboya, Medium, "The Oculus Go Wasn't Designed for Black Hair" https://debugger.medium.com/the-oculus-go-a-hard-ware-problem-for-black-women-225d9b48d098, published Nov 5, 2020.

or iPad to scan your face, ensuring a perfect fit, seal, and headband adjustment. Additionally, the optical customization feature accommodates prescription lenses directly in the headset, eliminating the need for additional glasses.

Haptic Feedback

Haptic feedback is a key element in comfort design for spatial design because it enhances immersion and realism by simulating tactile sensations, enabling more intuitive and natural interactions within the virtual environment. It helps reduce the reliance on visual cues, thereby decreasing cognitive load and visual fatigue. Haptic feedback also provides immediate, error-preventing feedback on user actions. It makes XR experiences more accessible to users with visual impairments, contributing to a more comfortable and engaging user experience.

Motion Movement

There are several common types of movement methods used in spatial design environments for different levels of immersion and comfort:

- **Teleportation:**
  - **How it Works:** Users point to a location and instantly teleport there.
  - **Best Practice:** Use visual indicators for possible teleport locations. Include a brief fade-in/fade-out effect to reduce disorientation.
  - **Advantages:** Greatly reduces motion sickness.[58] Quick and easy to use.
  - **Disadvantages:** Can break immersion.

- **Smooth Locomotion:**
  - **How it Works:** Users move continuously in the virtual environment, often using a joystick or touchpad.

---

[58] Centers for disease control and prevention(CDC), "Motion sickness happens when the movement you see is different from what your inner ear senses. This can cause dizziness, nausea, and vomiting." https://wwwnc.cdc.gov/travel/page/motion-sickness, accessed Jan. 2024.

- **Best Practice:** Implement adjustable speed settings and consider adding a "comfort mode" that includes a fixed reference point in the user's vision and darkens the surroundings while moving to reduce motion sickness.
- **Advantages:** Highly immersive; natural feeling of movement.
- **Disadvantages:** Can cause motion sickness in some users.

- **Arm-Swinging:**
  - **How it Works:** Users swing their arms to simulate walking, which triggers movement in the virtual environment. Gorilla Tag is a great example of using the arm-swinging movement.
  - **Best Practice:** Ensure the movement feels natural and corresponds well to the user's physical actions.
  - **Advantages:** Physically engaging; can feel more immersive and will be able to lose a lot of calories.
  - **Disadvantages:** Can be tiring and only applies some unique storytelling and gameplay; not suitable for all users or experiences.

- **Real Walking (Room-Scale):**
  - **How it Works:** Users physically walk in their play area, which is mapped to the virtual environment.
  - **Best Practice:** Indicate the boundaries of the play area and use techniques like "redirected walking" for larger virtual spaces.
  - **Advantages:** Highly immersive; natural and comfortable.
  - **Disadvantages:** Limited by physical space; not feasible for large virtual environments.

- **Vehicle-Based Movement:**
  - **How it Works:** Users control or ride in a virtual vehicle (like a car, spaceship, etc.).
  - **Best Practice:** Ensure smooth controls and provide a stable reference point within the vehicle to reduce motion sickness.
  - **Advantages:** Can cover large distances; adds variety to the experience.
  - **Disadvantages:** Requires additional design and control considerations.

The primary objective is to align your vision with the internal sensations from your inner ear and body, ensuring the brain receives harmonious signals. When traveling by car, it's recommended to sit in the front or beside a window, focus on the external view, refrain from reading or using digital devices, maintain a well-ventilated and cool environment inside the vehicle, and keep water and light snacks readily available. For a vehicle-based movement example, when the cable car moves inside Coco VR, it incorporates windows to minimize motion sickness. This virtual frame serves to distinguish between the 'Inside' and 'Outside' worlds, creating a stable reference point within the moving environment, much like the reassuring frame of a car window that prevents motion sickness by helping the brain differentiate between the vehicle's movement and the external surroundings. When moving it helps to darken the edge of the view to create a virtual frame to prevent motion sickness (i.e., tunnel vision comfort for locomotion).

Key Points for Movement Spatial Design:

1. **User Choice:** Offer multiple locomotion options, when possible, as user preference and comfort vary greatly.

Fig. 3.43: Coco VR uses a static frame to simulate being inside a vehicle, creating an illusion that aligns visual motion with physical stillness, thus preventing motion sickness.

2. **Gradual Introduction:** Gradually introduce movement mechanics, especially for new users.

3. **Stable Reference Points:** Provide stable reference points in the user's field of view to help with orientation and reduce motion sickness.

4. **Minimize Involuntary Movement:** Avoid sudden or involuntary movements as they can be disorienting or uncomfortable.

5. **Performance:** Ensure high and stable frame rates for smooth motion.

6. **Testing and Feedback:** Regularly test different locomotion methods with users and gather feedback to refine the experience.

Ultimately, the best practice for movement in spatial design depends on the specific application, the target audience, and the content of the experience. It's often beneficial to provide options and allow users to choose their preferred method of locomotion.

Mind Comfort

Visual Comfort

Opt for gentle, non-flickering lighting and a soothing, cohesive color scheme and simple texture and depth indication to avoid eye strain and discomfort. For Vision Pro, the immersive glass window enhances spatial awareness by providing a clear contrast with the external environment. It adjusts to changing light conditions and integrates harmoniously with its surroundings, ensuring visual comfort for the user.

Center Important Content within the Field of View

By default, visionOS initiates an app in front of the user, ensuring it's within their visual range. For longer interactions, it's crucial to maintain the content easily within their sight.

Dynamic Scale

Dynamic scaling ensures that content remains easily readable and interactive, irrespective of its distance from the user. VisionOS automatically enlarges a window's scale as it moves further from the wearer and reduces it as it approaches, creating the illusion that the window maintains a consistent size at every distance.

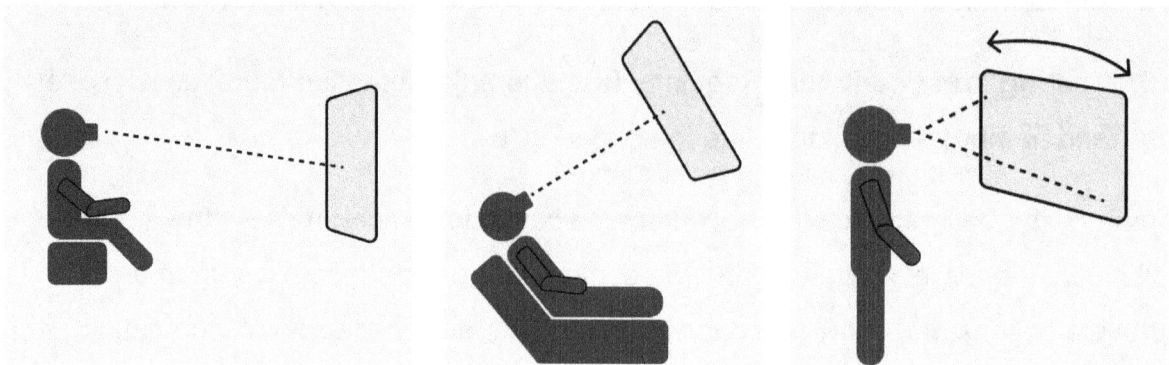

Fig. 3.44: Upright View: Content in the center of the user's view (Left). Angle View: Content in the center of the user's view (Center). Refrain from anchoring content to the user's head. Doing so can obstruct their view and detract from a comfortable experience (Right).

Fig. 3.45: Dynamic Scale: Enlarge the scale as the UI moves away from the user. Side view of the enlarged UI (Left). User's perspective (Right). This size adjustment helps the UI appear consistent with its original size, enhancing the user's comfort during the experience.

Comfortable UI Scale, Position, Timing, and Fonts

During a VR boxing game, I experienced motion sickness, dizziness, and nausea, which were exacerbated by the game's user interface. As the player focused on fighting the enemy, new combo instructions kept popping up, disrupting the player's flow, and causing distraction and dizziness, particularly during intense gameplay. This was frustrating as the player didn't know how to turn off these instructions, which the player didn't need.

Using all capital letters, especially during high-pressure moments that demand quick reactions, can impede readability, and disrupt player immersion. For instance, amid an urgent fight, it is difficult to quickly read through titles written entirely.

When creating a 2D UI experience in spatial, ensure the UI's scale, timing, position, and font are tailored to the gameplay to avoid visual discomfort. An obstructive UI, appearing when not needed, or titles and descriptions in all caps can increase cognitive load and hinder the gaming experience.

Audio Comfort

Fig. 3.46: Oversized Pop-Ups

To enhance immersion in virtual environments, use 3D spatial audio for environmental cues and ensure ambient sounds match the setting. It's important to avoid loud or sudden noises, adhering to the filmmaking principle that background music shouldn't overpower the scene. Audio can act as a navigational aid when visual cues are outside the field of view, subtly guiding users back on track for a cohesive immersive experience.

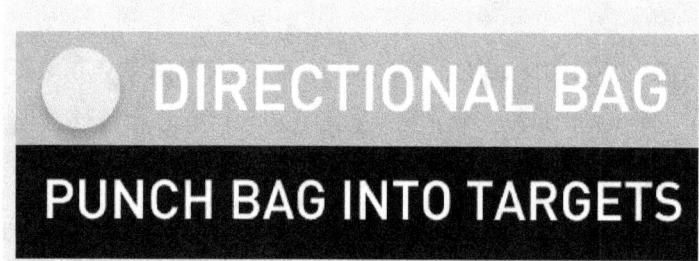

Fig. 3.47: Readability: Instructions in all capital letters can be challenging to read. The scenario is that this teaches players to quickly respond by punching the green bubbles. Lowercase instructions or icons can help speed up the action (Left). The UI is oversized and misplaced for the player to read. If read from a different angle, it is impossible to read the entire UI, and cannot see the entire instructions (Right).

Shared Space - Private, Collaborative, and Public

Paul Hoover, head of design at ShapesXR, stresses that understanding and catering to the diverse needs of users is crucial in designing virtual spaces for social interaction. The virtual world should provide something that people need, provide comfort, security, privacy, and social aspects. Good design in virtual environments serves a spectrum of purposes, from individual workspaces and collaborative areas to private and public rooms, catering to different groups such as creative individuals or business professionals. Paul suggests that successful virtual worlds are built upon the feedback of their intended audience, ensuring the space meets their specific demands for interaction, privacy, style, moderation, scheduling, and cross-platform compatibility.

Paul highlighted Figma as an excellent model for 2D collaboration, emphasizing its ability to offer different degrees of presence and synchronicity. The platform enables users to gain situational awareness by simply observing which documents others are engaging with and their current focus areas. Users can follow their colleagues to view their screen, join voice calls for real-time collaboration, or leave comments for asynchronous communication. These intuitive interactions mimic the natural dynamics of in-office teamwork. However, replicating this level of collaboration online demands significant engineering and design effort in spatial design.

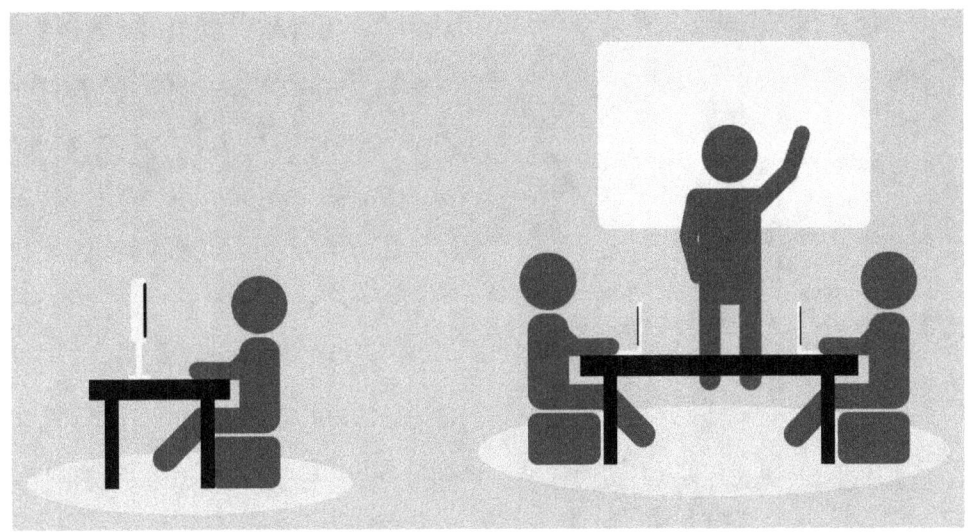

Fig. 3.48: A good collaboration tool should allow the designers to work solo or work together, and present as they wish, just like in the physical world office settings.

Scale in the Shared Space is Important

In the interview with Inga Petryaevskaya, CEO of ShapesXR, emphasized the importance of scale in spatial content within the Shared Space. While ShapesXR allows users to scale themselves dynamically during the creation process including collaborative creation process, they can easily scale back down to 1:1 scale, or "user scale", both via teleportation or by entering the play mode. It's very important to test content at 1:1 scale, to make sure that what the end user sees is correct. Improperly scaled interfaces will result in a negative experience.

Private and Public Space

In Vision Pro, the aim is to craft an immersive experience where "Everyone will see everyone else in the same relative position." This design philosophy ensures a uniform and cohesive user experience. Additionally, for the share screen/content feature, Vision Pro offers a variety of templates for developers. These templates are designed to guarantee "Visual Consistency," ensuring that all users view the same content within the app in a consistent manner.[59]

---

[59] Apple, https://developer.apple.com/videos/play/wwdc2023/10075, accessed Jan. 2024

Fig. 3.49: Vision Pro: Everyone is part of a meeting with a whiteboard presentation. (Source: Apple)

Vision Pro strives to emulate the group meeting dynamic, where everyone is part of a meeting with a whiteboard presentation. When someone points to the whiteboard, the platform ensures that all participants can see the action in its relative position, enhancing the collaborative experience. There are different scenarios for shared space such as side-by-side, conversational, and surround.

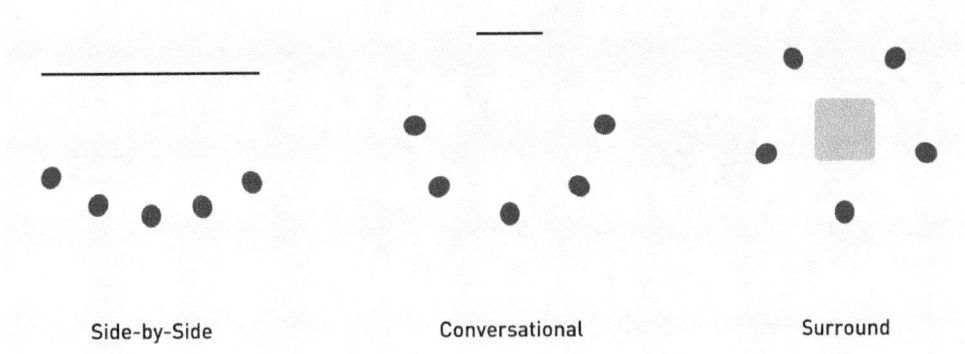

Fig. 3.50: Vision Pro: Side-by-Side, Conversational, and Surround. (Source: Apple)

Side-by-Side   Conversational   Surround

Fig. 3.51: Vision Pro: Participants have his/her individual controller to control the shared content. (Source: Apple)

Regarding the shared content, each participant can possess their own controller to independently manage the content. This enables participants to freely navigate and control the content without feeling restricted. Refer to Fig. 3.51 for more details.

In a shared space, if users are in different locations, icons will represent each user to prevent unexpected and unprepared disconnections that could distract the user.

In Fig. 3.52, On the right the perspective shifts to Joe's view. Here, Mary is similarly depicted as a 3D icon, distinctively void of her avatar form, as seen from Joe's perspective in their shared virtual environment. The illustration contrasts the two perspectives, highlighting the unique way everyone perceives each other in this digital realm. In this way, it preserves privacy for both users when the user is not ready to present in the virtual world or not in the same immersive space.

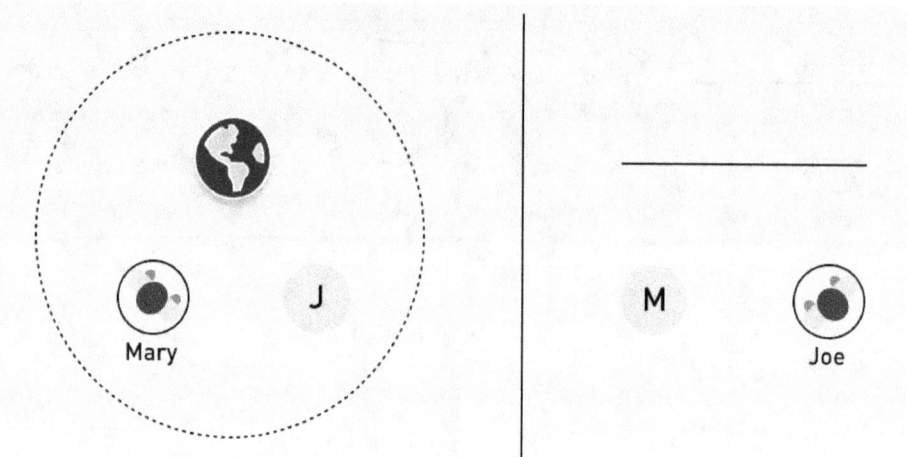

Fig. 3.52: Vision Pro: Right is looking at the 3D object: From Mary's perspective Joe is an icon to show Joe is absent. Left is looking at a UI or a 2D panel: From Joe's point of view, Mary is an icon to show her absence. (Source: Apple)

Conversely, if both users are in the same space, they will see each other as avatars within that space, allowing for direct interaction. Refer to Fig. 3.53 for more details.

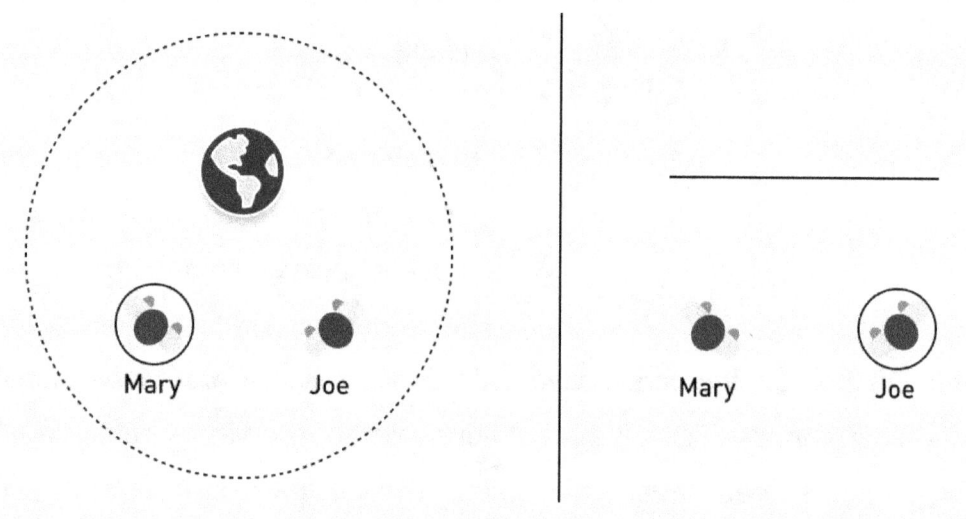

Fig. 3.53: Vision Pro: On the right side, both Mary and Joe are in the same immersive space. On the Left side, both Mary and Joe are in the same immersive space, but they can't see each other's avatars due to not being in the same space. (Source: Apple)

Building Blocks for Comfort

Components:	Actions:
Headset Comfort	• Headsets fits people of all kinds
Haptic Feedback	• Right proportion & Orientation • Comfortable Interactions
Motion Movement	• Teleportation • Smooth Locomotion • Arm-Swinging • Real Walking (Room-Scale) • Vehicle-Based Movement
Visual Comfort	• Avoid eye strain
Important Content	• The important content is within the user's visual range
Dynamic Scale	• content remains easily readable and interactive
Comfortable UI Scale, Position, Timing, and Fonts	• ensure the UI's scale, timing, position, and font are tailored to the gameplay
Audio Comfort	• 3D spatial audio
Shared Space - Private, Collaborate, and Present	• Separate private working space and collaborative working space.
Scale in the Share Space is important	• User Testing • Interactive Design

Reduce

"Less is more."
- Ludwig Mies van der Rohe

Key Design Patterns:

1. **Natural User Interface (NUI) Patterns:** Eye, hand, and Voice control.

2. **NUI & AI:** Provide immediate, error-preventing feedback on user actions and make XR experiences more accessible.

3. **Reduce Errors:** Create an "Undo" option, provide tutorials, and provide visual, sound, and haptic hints and feedback.

4. **Gesture Simplification:** Implement intuitive and natural gestures that mimic real-world interactions, reducing the need for complex control schemes.

5. **Focus on Core Interactions Prioritize Key Features:** Identify and develop the most critical interactions or experiences for your application, avoiding feature creep.

6. **Spatial Audio:** Use 3D spatial audio to guide users or provide feedback, which can be more intuitive and less visually intrusive than visual cues.

Why is Reduce Important?

Have you ever felt overwhelmed by an abundance of buttons on a webpage, uncertain about which one to press? This kind of confusion can become even more challenging in spatial computing, where navigating through a multitude of options turns into a daunting task. Unlike GUIs, which offer a structured approach with clear hierarchy and categorization, making navigation more manageable, spatial computing environments can sometimes be hard to find things you are looking for. They often require more logic, memory, and time to locate specific items.

On the other hand, Natural User Interfaces (NUI) offer a more personalized experience, allowing users to circumvent the laborious search process and directly access the information they seek. A prime illustration of this is the employment of AI personal assistants. These assistants can adeptly navigate users to the correct information or function, eliminating the need for manual exploration through various options.

What is Reduce?

In spatial computing, maintaining a simple UI and interaction design is crucial for enhancing user experience and accessibility. Simplified interfaces reduce cognitive load, making it easier for users to navigate and engage with the virtual environment, especially those new to spatial computing technology. This approach also ensures better performance and adaptability across various applications and devices. Additionally, a straightforward design helps keep users focused on the content rather than struggling with complex navigation, making the technology more approachable and enjoyable for a broader audience.

Natural User Interface (NUI)

"Until now, we have always had to adapt to the limits of technology and conform the way we work with computers to a set of arbitrary conventions and procedures. With NUI, computing devices will adapt to our needs and preferences for the first time and humans will begin to use technology in whatever way is most comfortable and natural for us." —Bill Gates

NUI is using a natural way to interact with the interface such as using eye, hand, and voice commands. It helps us interact with computers seamlessly and reduce the cognitive load due to it being the same interaction as we interact with the real-world.

Vision Pro finally gets rid of controllers by using eye-hand interactions. The eye-hand indirect gesture is efficient for UI and object interactions without controllers. The seamless natural way of interactions without the cognitive load of learning how to use the controller is efficient.

Leveraging spatial computing technology, users can interact directly with UI and objects using their hands. Eye gaze replaces traditional mouse hover and click actions based on gazing time, allowing for direct interaction after a certain duration. Gaze serves as a hover to display information, while hand gestures function as an indirect selection method, eliminating the need for learning gamepads/controllers and offering a more precise and intuitive experience, reducing cognitive load.

NUI and AI Interaction

In AWE USA 2023, David A Smith, CTO of Croquet Corporation, sparked an intriguing discussion about the future of AI. He proposed a scenario where, while wearing AR glasses and engaging in a conversation, the computer would be able to simulate and visualize the topic of discussion. For instance, if the conversation centered around a vacation destination, the computer would generate and visualize all its details, including shape, location, and size, to enhance understanding.

Fig. 3.54: People wearing AR glasses engage in conversations, during which a simulation is generated and changes dynamically according to the conversation. This assists the conversation by providing visualizations that correspond to the discussion topics.

With Vision Pro, when you look at something you can interact with, it gets highlighted. This highlight, like a mouse hover effect on a computer, tells you that the item is ready for action, like a tap. For instance, if you want to go back to a previous page in Chrome, simply look at the 'back' button and then tap it. Similarly, by looking at a photo, you can tap to view it in full. Sometimes, Vision Pro does more than just highlight. If you gaze at a tab bar, it might enlarge, showing labels next to the tabs. Before the whole bar gets bigger, the tab you're looking at will light up first, allowing you to pick it. Additionally, some buttons might show extra information or a message when you focus on them.

Apple's recent unveiling of Ferret,[60] a new AI system, marks a significant leap in the field of multimodal artificial intelligence. Outperforming GPT-4 in key computer vision tasks, Ferret excels in analyzing both visual and textual data, particularly in identifying and describing intricate details within complex images. This advancement showcases Apple's focus on enhancing detailed visual comprehension and sets a new standard in multimodal AI. Ferret's introduction not only signals a major shift in Apple's AI strategy, potentially impacting products like Siri and iOS, but also intensifies the competition in

---

[60] Ferret Github, https://github.com/apple/ml-ferret, accessed Feb. 2024.

the AI industry, especially in areas of computer vision and natural language processing. By integrating with Ferret, Vision Pro will be able to use voice commands to synchronously generate visual simulations while having conversations. Spatial computing combined with powerful AI will seamlessly bridge the gap between ideas to execution.

NUI Design Patterns

Leveraging technological advancements like sensors, computer vision, and artificial intelligence, users can experience more while doing less, resulting in a more engaging interaction. Unlike the traditional 2D screen experience governed by Graphical User Interfaces (GUIs), spatial design integrates Natural User Interfaces (NUIs). These interfaces are more direct and intuitive, utilizing voice, eye, and hand movements to foster intuitive interactions. The key feature of spatial design is its ultra-low friction and effortless user experience, ensuring seamless engagement with digital environments.

Here are some examples of ultra-low friction user interfaces:

1. **Gaze-Based Interactions:** Instead of needing to use hand controllers or buttons, many new devices use eye tracking to establish what the user is looking at. When the user looks at a UI element it subtly highlights. To select, the user can hold their gaze on that object or tap two fingers together.

2. **Voice Command Integration:** A user can simply speak their intent, for example, in the more recent Meta Quest headsets the user can speak a phrase like "Start Recording", and the video will immediately begin to record without the need to engage with any physical controls - thus leaving their hands entirely free for other activities.

3. **Real-time Hand Tracking:** Systems such as Vision Pro, Meta Quest 3, and HoloLens 2 can track individual finger movements without the need for external controllers, allowing users to interact with objects in the virtual space as they

would in the real world, or use specific gestures such as "pinch" or "swipe" as a user interface like those used with touch screen technologies.

4. **Adaptive Environments:** The digital environment maps to the user's physical movement without any additional input. For example, when a user walks closer to a virtual object it might provide more detailed information or change its behavior.

5. **Avatar Realism & Natural Language Conversation powered by AI:** In a virtual social gathering, the user's avatar may automatically mimic their real-world body language and facial expressions, making social interactions look and feel more natural. In EngageVR, Athena AI is a virtual assistant that not only assists the user through natural language conversation but also generates images and skyboxes powered by Open AI. Athena is being designed as a solution for enterprises and will be used for employee onboarding, sales calls, education, training, and much more.

For Avatar Realism, Meta announced *Pixel Codec Avatars.*[61] On the Sept. 28 episode of the *Lex Fridman Podcast,*[62] Zuckerberg and Lex had an hour-long discussion. Their entire conversation took place using lifelike avatars in the metaverse, enabled by Quest Pro headsets and noise-canceling headphones. SapientXR specializes in creating and customizing digital humans designed to assist people in various settings.

For instance, at trade shows these digital humans can exist on vertical display screens, performing roles such as welcoming and assisting attendees. They can act as interactive guides, allowing visitors to inquire about specific booths or ongoing keynote events. Through a combination of computer vision and AI, these digital beings interact with users in real time. Incorporating a human-like form and facial expressions, especially in voice-command applications, is crucial for roles like greeters, front desk assistants, and medical aides. This humanized approach aims to provide a warm and

---

[61] Meta, https://research.facebook.com/publications/pixel-codec-avatars, accessed Jan. 2024.
[62] Lex Fridman, https://www.youtube.com/watch?v=MVYrJJNdrEg, accessed Jan. 2024.

welcoming experience, enhancing the feeling of personal interaction and comfort in settings like hospitals and customer service desks.

Numerous Eye Tracking and Hand Interaction features are available in MRTK 2 and MRTK 3, Vision Pro, Meta Quest building blocks, and through various UX documentation. Below are some examples of the existing hand interaction patterns:

Indirect Gestures

An indirect gesture influences the object that people are focused on. For instance, if people are observing a button, visionOS[63] emphasizes it, offering a visual indication that it can be activated. They can perform this activation by rapidly tapping their finger to their thumb and executing the indirect tap gesture.

Indirect gestures are typically quick, as people can rapidly shift their gaze in various

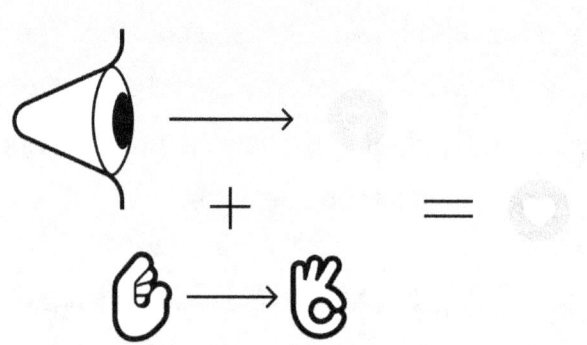

directions, and they are comfortable since device cameras can detect hand movements even when hands are resting on laps or hanging at the sides. Moreover, these gestures allow interaction with any object in view, irrespective of its spatial location, eliminating the need for physical reach.

Fig. 3.55: Indirect Gestures: Eye-Hand Gestures: Fast and comfortable. (Source: Apple)

---

[63] Apple, https://developer.apple.com/design/human-interface-guidelines/designing-for-visionos, accessed Jan. 2024.

Direct Interaction

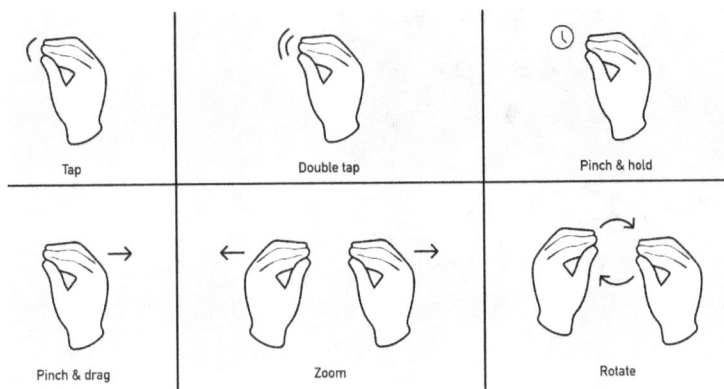

Fig. 3.56: Direct Gestures. (Source: Apple)

A direct gesture impacts the object that individuals are physically interacting with. In visionOS, this means virtually touching an object by bringing a finger close to it. For instance, users can engage with the system-provided keyboard by touching the keys. Direct gestures necessitate objects being within arm's reach. Additionally, as these gestures involve moving the hand towards the object rather than just the eyes, they are more suitable for scenarios where rapid and precise interactions are not essential.

Volumetric Buttons

Volumetric buttons are versatile buttons designed for various input modalities, such as poking, gaze-pinch, ray interactions, mouse clicks, and gamepad inputs. (Source: MRTK[64])

---

[64] Microsoft, https://learn.microsoft.com/en-us/windows/mixed-reality/mrtk-unity/mrtk3-overview, accessed Jan. 2024

Fig. 3.57: Volumetric button designed for various input modalities, such as poking, gaze-pinch, ray interactions, mouse clicks, and gamepad inputs. (Source: MRTK)

Hand Menu

Hand menu is a hand-anchored collection of UX controls for easy access to quick actions. It normally requires either a flip of gaze to trigger the hand menu and the other hand to poke/direct interaction to select. (Source: MRTK)

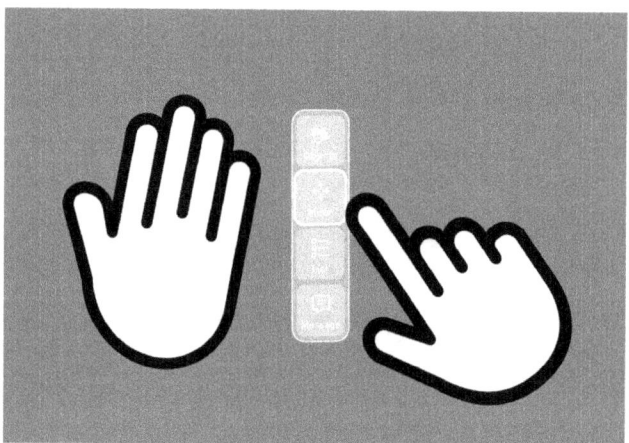

Fig. 3.60: A hand-anchored collection of UX controls for easy access to quick actions. (Source: MRTK)

Near Menu

A near menu is a prevalent pattern featuring a set of manipulable UI elements that can be moved and adjusted to follow the user. Users have the option to world-lock/unlock the menu using the 'Pin' button. The menu is easily grabbed and positioned at a specific location within the world, enhancing user flexibility.

Fig. 3.61: The Near Menu is a prevalent pattern featuring a set of manipulable UI elements that can be moved and adjusted to follow the user. (Source: MRTK)

Virtual Keyboard

A virtual keyboard helps reduce time and effort by direct hand type instead of triggering each key through controllers. Virtual keyboards in platforms like Meta Quest, Microsoft's Mixed Reality Toolkit (MRTK), and Apple Vision Pro exemplify the advancements in text input within virtual, augmented, and mixed reality environments. Meta Quest leverages hand tracking and controllers for typing, enhancing VR immersion with a 3D floating keyboard. MRTK supports spatial interaction and controller input across various MR devices, including HoloLens, incorporating voice commands for added convenience. Apple Vision Pro, while newer to the scene, is anticipated to integrate sophisticated hand tracking and gesture recognition, along with seamless voice-to-text capabilities, leveraging Apple's ecosystem for a user-friendly virtual keyboard experience. These platforms collectively push the boundaries of digital interaction, making virtual text input more intuitive and accessible across different devices and user preferences.

Fig. 3.62: Helps reduce time and effort by direct hand type instead of triggering each key through controllers. (Source: MRTK)

Here are several Natural User Interface (NUI) objects that can be interacted with in various ways, including manipulation by bounds, direct grabbing, scaling, pointing, distant grabbing, raycasting interaction, throwing, and more.

Bounds

Bounds provide an automatically sized bounding box, along with manipulation affordances for rotation and scale.

Fig. 3.58: Provide an automatically sized bounding box, along with manipulation affordances for rotation and scale. (Source: MRTK)

Direct Manipulate Objects with Hands

The user can move and manipulate objects with one or two hands. More specifically, rotate, scale, move, and more directly manipulate the 3D object. This method of manipulation is highly intuitive and mimics the way we interact with physical objects in the real world, making it easier for users to learn and use. It enhances the sense of immersion and presence within a virtual environment, key factors in the effectiveness and enjoyment of VR and AR experiences. Moreover, it allows for precise control over digital objects, essential for applications requiring detailed manipulation, such as design, education, and medical simulations.

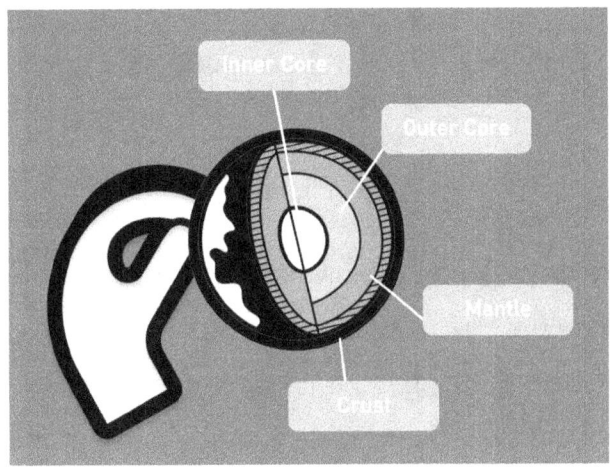

Fig. 3.59: Move and manipulate objects with one or two hands. (Source: MRTK)

Pointable Item

The "Pointable Item" feature in Meta Quest 3 enhances virtual interaction by allowing users to point at objects with their hands for remote engagement, leveraging advanced hand tracking and gesture recognition technology. This intuitive control method simplifies the user interface, making virtual environments more accessible and engaging. By enabling users to interact with items from a distance, it opens new possibilities for application in gaming, education, and virtual meetings, ensuring a more inclusive and user-friendly experience. This feature exemplifies the focus on natural and immersive interactions within the Meta Quest ecosystem.

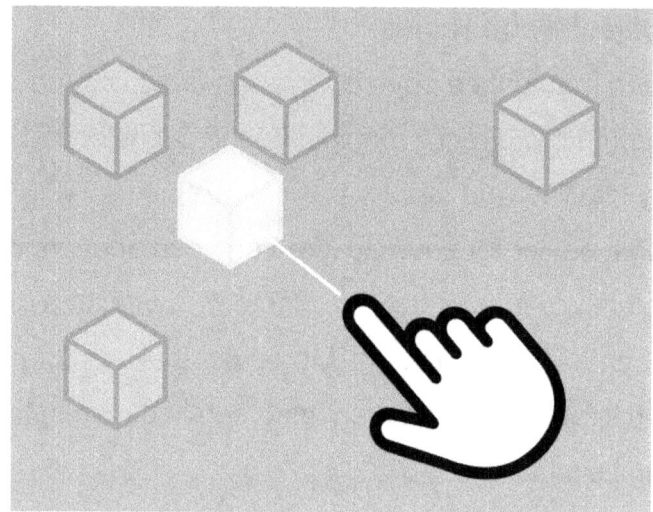

Fig. 3.63: Pointable item for distance selection and interactions. (Source: Meta)

Throwable Item

The "Throwable Item" feature in the Meta Quest Unity ecosystem enables developers to create immersive VR experiences by allowing virtual objects to be interacted with in a realistic manner—picked up, held, and thrown by users. Leveraging Unity's physics engine and the Meta Quest SDK's hand tracking capabilities, this feature ensures objects behave as expected when thrown, enhancing realism and user engagement. It's especially beneficial in games and simulations where accurate object dynamics are critical, providing a more interactive and enjoyable experience. Developers must balance realism with playability, incorporating feedback mechanisms like visual and audio cues to enrich the sense of interaction and immersion within the virtual environment.

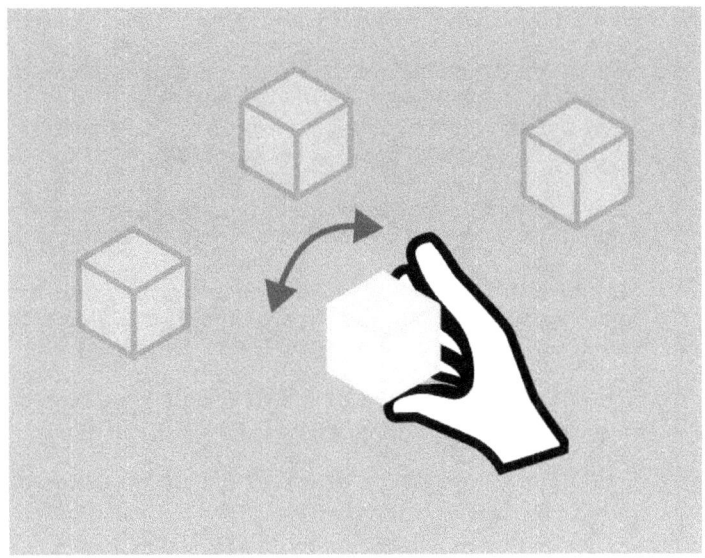

Fig. 3.64: Throwable item for certain interactions such as darts, golfing, and waving hands.
(Source: Meta)

Surface Projection Passthrough

The "Surface Projection Passthrough" feature in Meta Quest 3, integrated with Unity, marks a leap in MR by allowing developers to overlay virtual content onto real-world surfaces through the headset's passthrough cameras. This technology blends digital objects with the user's physical environment in real-time, enabling applications to interact with actual space, enhancing immersion and interactivity. Ideal for gaming, education, and interior design, it necessitates careful design to ensure seamless integration of virtual and real elements, addressing challenges like lighting, object permanence, and user safety. This building block opens innovative possibilities for creating more engaging and interactive VR experiences.

Fig. 3.65: Surface Projection Passthrough: to see magical reality. Can apply to different types of simulations and storytelling. (Source: Meta)

Hand Gestures

Robin Moulder and Chris Castaldi, alongside other members of the development team at 3lbGames,[65] have created a game called Grokit, which operates on the innovative premise that future gaming may not require traditional controllers. Grokit allows players to engage through simple hand gestures. Robin envisions a future where conventional controllers are phased out, giving way to intuitive hand gestures and signs for gameplay. Chris anticipates the integration of minimalist devices, such as a pen-like tool or a single-button controller, to complement hand gestures where more precise interaction is necessary.

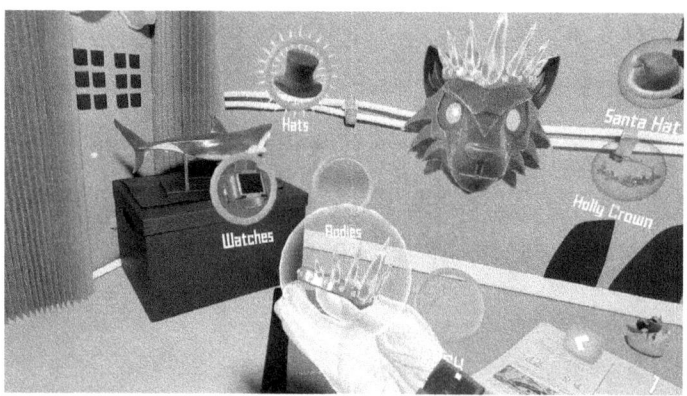

Fig. 3.66: The Grokit game allows the users to grab the 3D Object to select. (Source: Grokit)

---

[65] 3lbGames, https://3lbgames.com/grokit, accessed Jan. 2024

Grokit features both single-player and multiplayer modes, offering extensive customization options for avatars, hands, and themes. The gameplay involves straightforward hand interactions that transform players' hands into various shapes, like cat paws, sharks, or even simulate shooting actions. The creation of such seamless hand tracking is a remarkable feat considering the complexity of accurately tracking hand movements. Chris elaborates on the challenges faced during the development of the gesture tracking system, noting the diversity in how individuals grasp objects — some with thumbs outstretched, others with thumbs tucked, and even others using a claw-like gesture.

Fig. 3.67: Grokit turns players' hands into sharks to bite the fish and gain points. (Source: Grokit)

To accommodate this variety of grips and positions, the Grokit team has engineered a robust gesture tracking infrastructure. Moreover, Grokit's success in hand tracking has led to the development of the GroKit Core platform under 3lbXR, a toolkit that empowers creators to craft hand tracking, MR, and multiplayer applications without the need to code from scratch. This enables creators to focus solely on the conceptual aspect of hand tracking, without the burden of reinventing the gesture-recognition system. The GroKit Core platform solutions are designed to propel all industry verticals, enhancing the application of XR in tangible scenarios. With the promise of increased project efficiency, reduced costs, and access to high-quality code libraries, GroKit Core is committed to laying down the fundamental infrastructure for businesses intent on excelling in spatial computing.

Grokit Core is a spatial computing development platform for MR and VR applications that offers a full-code development platform with low code features, simplifying the creation of immersive experiences. With features like customizable preconfigured components (GroBlocks), advanced AI integrations, intuitive hand tracking, scene understanding, multiplayer support, and cross-platform compatibility, it empowers developers to quickly prototype and deploy innovative XR applications. Whether you're an experienced developer or new to XR, GroKit Core provides the tools, AI assistance, and prototype assets needed to push the boundaries of spatial computing and generative AI, making groundbreaking applications more accessible than ever.

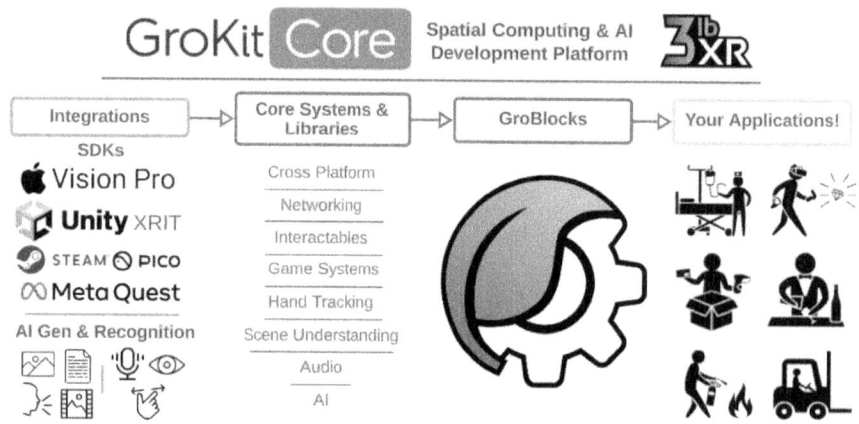

Fig. 3.68: GroKit Core is an integrated platform offering a suite of tools, AI assistance, and prototype assets designed to advance spatial computing and generative AI, thereby democratizing the development of cutting-edge applications. (Source: Grokit)

Another example is "The Wizards - Dark Times: Brotherhood," where players use hand gestures in VR to cast spells and create weapons. The game tracks hand movements with VR controllers, allowing players to mimic actions like throwing fireballs or shaping weapons. This game merges gestures for more potent spells, enhancing immersion through natural movements. Mastery is achieved through practice and refinement in combat, object manipulation, and world interaction.

Fig. 3.69: The Wizards - Dark Times: Brotherhood:
Players use gestures and movements to conjure spells
and wield weapons.

Waist Menu

Functioning like a digital watch, this feature delivers a straightforward, accessible, and swift way to reach shortcuts, thereby improving the user experience through its efficiency and user-friendly design.

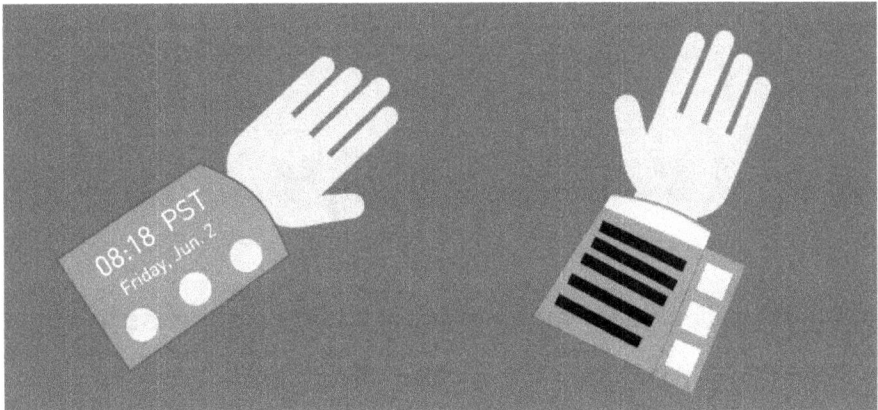

Fig. 3.70: Hand face down (Left). Hand face up (Right). The hand or wrist
menu provides users with quick and easy access to key functions and
shortcuts. This design eliminates the need to navigate through a larger home
panel to find specific options. Serving as a virtual watch, this feature offers a
simple, convenient, and rapid means of accessing shortcuts.

Voice command

David Colleen at SapientX mentioned that as for the voice command, normally the users are "Very young" and "Very old", for the younger people, talking is more natural for them instead of typing. As for elders, the eyes start becoming blurry when seeing things, so speaking will be the easiest way to make a command for the elders.

Other Ways to Reduce

Avoid Displaying Unorganized Windows

An excess of windows can overwhelm and confine the user, potentially leading to discomfort. Maintain a simple UI, embracing the principle that less is more.

Fig. 3.71: Displaying an excessive number of windows can confine the user, leading to discomfort.

Organize all the information into a single window and use tab views to toggle between different data sets, thereby reducing the number of windows.

Focus on Essential Elements

For instance, in FitXR, when players follow the virtual coach, a minimalistic UI displays only the necessary combos and a profile icon with a countdown timer, avoiding any unnecessary information that might divert attention. Consequently, players can concentrate on their workout and their movements, ensuring a focused and undisturbed experience.

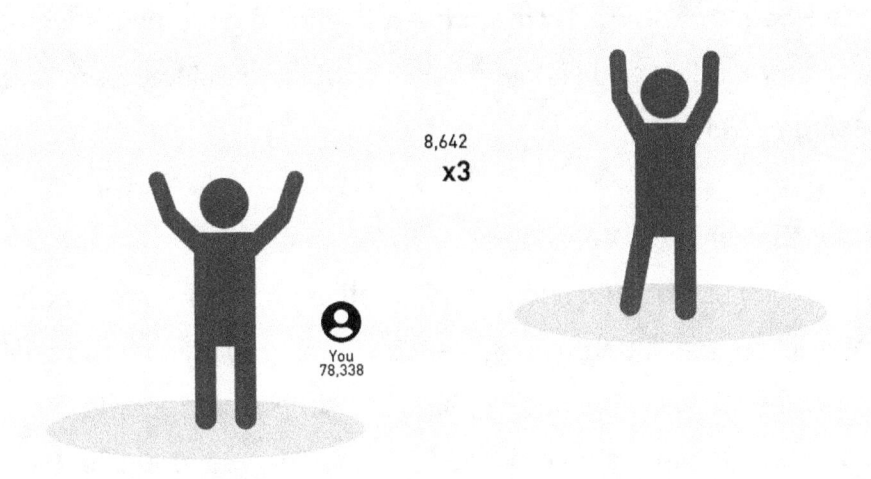

Fig. 3.72: Use simple graphics to indicate winning points, status, and time.

Enhanced Aesthetics

Clean and uncluttered designs are often more visually appealing, which can improve user engagement and satisfaction.

Performance Optimization

In spatial design, heavy graphics, and complex interactions can lead to performance issues. A minimalist design can help optimize performance, ensuring a smoother experience without lags or glitches. Here are some ways for you to optimize the performance:

- **Optimize Asset Sizes**: Ensure that the asset sizes are as small as possible without compromising quality.

- **Use Baked Lighting:** Where possible, use baked lighting instead of real-time to save on processing power.

- **Efficient Shading:** Write efficient shaders and consider using simpler shader models for mobile or lower-end devices.

- **Simplify Geometry:** Use simpler geometry for background objects.

- **Balance Realism and Performance Art Style:** Choose an art style that allows for lower poly models and simpler textures, which can look great and require less processing power.

Limitations can Encourage Creativity

Limiting elements can sometimes encourage creative problem-solving both in design and in user interaction, leading to innovative ways of engaging with the environment. For example, in *Workrooms*,[66] instead of using the controller trigger to draw on the board, the user needs to flip the controller and draw. The way of using the controller is innovative without extra memory to remember which button to press.

Down to the Rabbit Hole[67] is a VR game that introduces a unique narrative style, reimagining the classic tale of Alice in Wonderland. The gameplay confines the player to a small dollhouse space, allowing for 360-degree rotation to look up, down, and around, following the story. While the game's physical space isn't extensive and lacks elaborate action sequences, it creates a deeply immersive dollhouse experience.

The story unfolds interactively for the player, with UI elements appearing in a way that seamlessly integrates them into the narrative's progression. The game is reminiscent of a Wes Anderson movie, employing dollhouse aesthetics to narratively unfold the entire plot. This interactive design is perfectly tailored for VR, where players are immersed in a gradual descent, peeking in, and controlling the main character to solve puzzles.

---

[66] https://forwork.meta.com/horizon-workrooms/

[67] https://www.meta.com/experiences/2476104599150595/

Reduce Errors

"An ounce of prevention is worth a pound of cure." -Benjamin Franklin

Reliable and error-free spatial design experiences build user trust, crucial for the technology's adoption and ongoing use. In educational or training applications, minimizing errors is essential for effective learning and skill acquisition. From a commercial perspective, error prevention is vital for protecting brand reputation and avoiding financial losses. It also reduces the need for post-launch troubleshooting and maintenance, saving resources. Moreover, in sectors like healthcare or industry, error prevention in spatial design has significant legal and ethical implications, highlighting its importance across various applications.

The mixed reality game Pillow features enhances the user experience by encouraging relaxation. Players are prompted to lie down on a bed to engage in the game. If the player is sitting or standing, a transparent UI gently reminds them to lie down, ensuring it doesn't obstruct their view. The UI employs a calming font, contributing to the overall well-crafted design of the game. For apps that rely on hand tracking, it's crucial to have a system in place to inform users when there are issues with Wi-Fi or tracking functionality. This can help prevent unintended gestures, like throwing objects or waving, which might lead to frame latency and result in nausea. Implementing a notification or alert system within the app can guide users to avoid actions

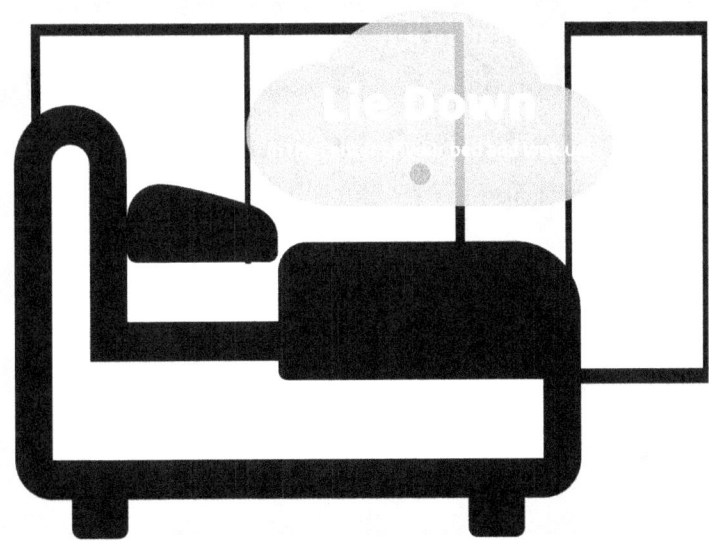

Fig. 3.73: Pillow. In the Pillow mixed-reality game, If the player is sitting or standing, a transparent UI gently reminds them to lie down on the bed, ensuring it doesn't obstruct their view.

that could disrupt the smooth functioning of the application due to connectivity or tracking problems.

Fig. 3.74: Warning graphics. The system displays red hands warning graphics or notifications to alert users and prevent potential errors.

Avoid Making Crucial Mistakes in Decision-Making:

- **Undo Options:** Many apps include an "undo" feature, allowing users to easily revert actions. This is particularly useful in creative or design-oriented apps, where users might make unintended changes to their creations.

- **Voice or Visual Confirmations:** In applications that use voice commands, confirmation prompts are often used. For instance, if a user verbally instructs the game to perform an action (e.g., "delete this item"), the app might ask for verbal confirmation to prevent accidental deletions.

Fig. 3.75: Confirmation pop-up. Add extra confirmation steps for significant actions, like irreversible deletion of important items, to prevent accidental data loss.

- **Gesture Recognition Thresholds:** To prevent accidental inputs, applications often set thresholds for gesture recognition. For example, a VR drawing app might require a certain level of precision or a specific gesture duration to ensure that the input is intentional. Some games adjust control sensitivity based on the context. For instance, in a VR shooting game, the trigger might require a firmer press during high-stakes moments to prevent accidental firing.

- **Content UI is Distinct from the System UI:** Ensure that the design of the app's UI is distinctly different from that of the System UI. If the design styles are too similar, users might become confused, and uncertain whether they are interacting with elements at the game level or the system level.

- **Clear and Consistent UI Elements:** Clear and consistently designed UI elements help prevent user errors. For example, ensuring that interactive elements are easily distinguishable and that their functions are obvious can significantly reduce accidental inputs.

Building Blocks for Reduce

Components:	Actions:
Cognitive Load Reduction & Focus on Essential Elements	• Less is more
Enhanced Aesthetics	• Clean and uncluttered designs
Performance Optimization	• Optimize Asset Size • Use Baked Lighting • Efficient Shading • Optimize Scripts • Simplify Geometry
Emphasis on Immersion and storytelling	• Focusing the narrative
Scalability and Flexibility	• Be easily adapted and expanded
Limitation Can Encourage Creativity	• Innovative ways of engaging with the environment
Avoid Make Unintended Changes	• Undo Option
Avoid Control and Game Play Errors	• Tutorials • Guidance (Visual & Sound Cue)
Avoid making crucial mistakes in decision-making	• Voice or Visual Confirmation
Prevent Accidentally Inputs	• Gesture Recognition Threshold
Immediately understand the consequence of the action	• Visual and Auditory Feedback

Minimize confusion between game-level and system-level controls	• Ensure that the UI design distinctly varies between the system and game levels
Reduce Accidental Inputs	• Clear & Consistent UI
Gesture Simplification	• Implement intuitive and natural gestures that mimic real-world interactions
3D Spatial Audio	• 3D spatial audio to guide users or provide feedback

Personalize

"Be yourself. Everyone else is already taken."
-Oscar Wilde

Key Design Patterns:

1. **User Profiling and Data Analysis:** Collect and analyze user data to understand individual preferences, behaviors, and needs.

2. **Adaptive Content and Interfaces:** Design XR and spatial computing systems to dynamically adapt content and interfaces based on user profiles. This could mean altering visual elements, changing interaction modes, or customizing information presentation based on the user's history, preferences, or even real-time reactions.

3. **Context-Aware Computing:** Leverage sensors to make XR environments context-aware. This means the system can understand and respond to the physical environment, user location, time of day, or even emotional states, adjusting the experience accordingly.

4. **AI Assistant:** Provide AI assistant to help the users.

5. **Avatar Personalization:** Involve users in the design process through user testing, feedback loops, and co-creation sessions. This ensures that the designs are closely aligned with actual user needs and preferences.

6. **Accessibility and Inclusivity Features:** Incorporate features that cater to a wide range of abilities, such as adjustable text sizes, contrast settings, audio descriptions, and gesture-based controls in spatial computing environments. This makes the system accessible and usable for all users.

Why is Personalization Important?

The 2023 Roblox Digital Expressions Report[68] emphasized that Digital identity is increasingly eclipsing physical appearance for Gen Z, with a majority valuing their virtual avatars' style above their real-world look. Avatar customization and digital fashion are important. These virtual styles are not just about aesthetics; they're integral to personal expression and psychological health, influencing real-life fashion choices and underscoring the significance of brands in the metaverse.

Personalization significantly enhances user experience by tailoring spaces and interactions to individual needs and preferences. This approach not only ensures greater accessibility and inclusivity but also fosters a deeper emotional connection and engagement. Additionally, it enhances learning and productivity in educational and professional settings, offers unique business and marketing opportunities, and future-proof designs in an ever-evolving technological landscape. Ultimately, personalization leads to more effective, engaging, and user-friendly environments and experiences.

What is Personalization?

Personalization in XR and spatial computing involves tailoring these technologies to individual user preferences and behaviors, enhancing the experience across various applications. For example, in education, VR can adjust to a student's learning pace, while in retail, AR apps might recommend products based on past purchases. In healthcare, personalized VR scenarios can aid in patient treatment and rehabilitation. In entertainment, XR environments can change according to a user's gameplay style or choices, and in the workplace, virtual meetings can be customized for each participant's role, showcasing the versatility and user-centric focus of these technologies.

---

[68] Roblox, https://blog.roblox.com/wp-content/uploads/2023/11/2023-Roblox-Digital-Expressions-Report.pdf?utm_source=blog&utm_medium=pdf+download&utm_campaign=digital+expressions, accessed Jan. 2024

How to Create Personalization?

In spatial computing, personalization is achieved by collecting and analyzing user data to create profiles that inform dynamic content and interface adjustments. Systems leverage AI and machine learning to adapt in real-time to individual behaviors, preferences, and context, such as physical surroundings and emotional states, enhancing accessibility and user experience. Features like eye-tracking allow for efficient resource allocation, enhancing performance, while avatar customization, accessibility options, and modular designs ensure inclusivity and adaptability to a wide array of user needs. These strategies collectively create a personalized and immersive experience for each user.

User Profiling and Data Analysis

To order the Apple Vision Pro, a customer must first perform a facial scan using an iPhone or iPad equipped with Face ID.[69] This step allows Apple to tailor the Light Seal and Headband for a personalized fit. For those who wish to use the Vision Pro without their glasses, an up-to-date prescription must be uploaded during the ordering process. The onboarding process includes a set of tests designed to calibrate the headset to the user's unique eye movements and to evaluate the contrast sensitivity against various backgrounds. This ensures that the Vision Pro can accurately facilitate eye-hand coordination indirectly, enhancing the user experience.

In one of the M1@M1Astra posts on X, *"Your eyes and hands are how you navigate Apple Vision Pro. You browse the system by looking, and it responds to your eyes. Simply look at an element and tap your fingers together to select it. It's like a click on*

---

[69] Apple, "Face ID provides intuitive and secure authentication enabled by the state-of-the-art TrueDepth camera system with advanced technologies to accurately map the geometry of your face." https://support.apple.com/en-us/102381#:~:text=Face%20ID%20provides%20intuitive%20and,your%20iPhone%20or%20iPad%20Pro. , accessed Jan. 2024.

your Mac. To scroll, pinch your fingers together, and gently flick. You can keep your hands where they're comfortable, such as resting on your lap."[70]

Vision Pro seamlessly integrates diverse user requirements, beginning with the adjustment of the headset to fit the unique contours of the user's face. By gathering and analyzing user data, it enables precise, natural eye-hand interactions, resulting in a fully immersive experience that feels intuitive and personalized for everyone.

Contextual-Awareness Design

Contextual awareness requires the designer to understand the environment. The design needs to function well regardless of if it is 2D, 2.5D, or 3D. Meta Quest 3 employs advanced room mesh scanning for context-aware computing, a feature that enhances XR experiences by creating a detailed 3D map of the user's environment. This technology allows the headset to understand and interact with physical space, adapting XR content dynamically to the surroundings. For example, the design of the mixed-reality app might require more user testing. Thomas Van Bouwel mentioned when he was developing the Laser Dance mixed-reality game, he asked users to upload the room scans to him so he could simulate different scenarios of rooms to make sure the game could map successfully with everyone's room.

In Apple Vision Pro, the choice of tool depends on the design's dimensionality and desired depth. For flat or 2D designs, opt for Windows to present your content in a straightforward, traditional manner. If your content is a 3D object or you aim to enhance it with depth, Volumes are the ideal choice, providing a more dynamic, three-dimensional presentation. For a completely immersive experience, where you wish to envelop users in your content, Spaces are the go-to option, offering an expansive and engaging environment.

---

[70] M1@M1Astra, https://x.com/M1Astra/status/1724506943425757367?s=20, accessed Jan. 2024.

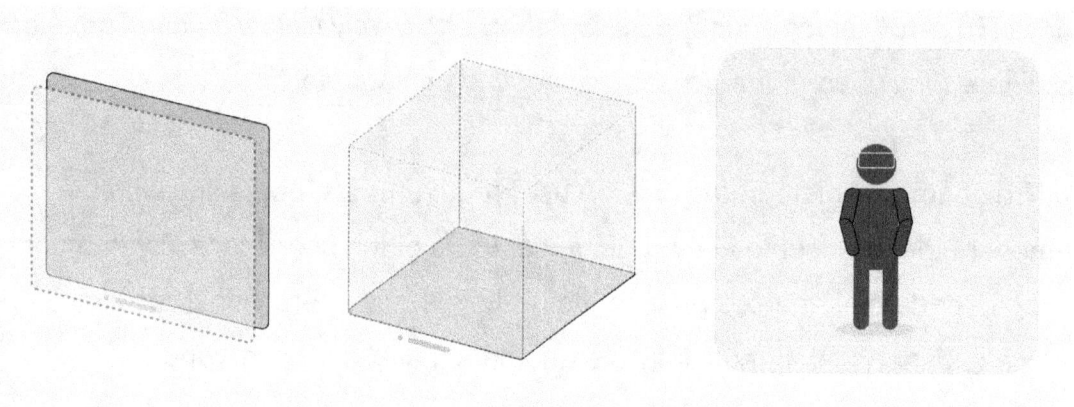

Fig. 3.76: From left to right: Windows, Volumes, and Spaces.

AI Assistant

Engage VR recently unveiled Athena AI, a cutting-edge development by the Engage AI team. This innovative AI, built upon the foundations of ChatGPT and DALL-E, is designed to interact uniquely with users. Athena has the remarkable ability to generate images that mirror her emotions and to respond to user inquiries. Currently, Engage VR is in the process of integrating Athena with our enterprise clients, initiating a series of pioneering projects. These endeavors are set to showcase the immense possibilities that arise from merging AI technology, including spatial computing and immersive technologies, to create a more dynamic and interactive user experience.

Avatar Personalization

According to Roblox's report Gen Z[71] cared about their digital avatar more than their physical appearance. Avatar personalization in XR and spatial computing is pivotal for enhancing user immersion, enabling self-expression, and facilitating social interaction. By allowing users to tailor their digital representations, it promotes a sense of presence and identity within virtual environments. This customization also supports inclusivity, allowing for diverse and accessible character designs that reflect the real-world variety

---

[71] Roblox, https://blog.roblox.com/wp-content/uploads/2023/11/2023-Roblox-Digital-Expressions-Report.pdf?utm_source=blog&utm_medium=pdf+download&utm_campaign=digital+expressions, accessed Jan. 2024

of users. Furthermore, in professional settings, personalized avatars can embody brand identities and aid in role-specific tasks, while in social and gaming contexts, they enrich communication and personal connections.

Jim Conrad, Senior Designer at Mozilla Hubs and formerly at Altspace, has expressed that the internet, particularly through WebXR, offers a unique opportunity for individuals to explore and experiment with different personas and identities. He likens this to a 'wild west' of exciting possibilities. In contrast, Mark Zuckerberg, CEO of Meta, has a differing view, stating, "...Having two identities for yourself is an example of a lack of integrity."

These contrasting viewpoints significantly influence the result of their respective products. Meta Horizon Worlds tend to feature avatars with a consistent 3D style, offering detailed customization options, but overall, the avatar style is the same. On the other hand, Mozilla Hubs goes a step further in personalization by allowing users to upload custom avatars. The partnership with ReadyPlayerMe further expands the range of options available to users, offering a broader scope for identity expression and experimentation.

Unifying online identities can enhance safety, creating a consistent digital presence. However, this uniformity could constrain the explorative and imaginative aspects of digital worlds, turning play into a chore. Echoing Jim Conrad's observations, our multifaceted lives see us adopt varied personas in interactions with children, spouses, friends, and colleagues. A singular identity might not capture the richness of these diverse roles.

Other Personalized Settings

Common Settings:

    1. **Audio Settings:**

- Volume Controls: Separate sliders for background music, SFX, and voice.
- Audio Effects: Enable or disable specific audio effects like reverb or echo.
- Voice Chat: Toggle voice chat on or off, with microphone sensitivity settings.

2. **Control Customization:**
   - Button Mapping: Allow users to remap controller buttons for their preferred actions.
   - Field of View (FOV): Let users change the FOV to suit their comfort level.
   - Dominant Hand: Let users choose their dominant hand for gameplay.
   - Sensitivity: Adjust the controller sensitivity for precise movements.

3. **Movement Options:**
   - Locomotion Style: Offer options like teleportation, smooth movement, teleportation, room-scale, vehicle style movement... etc.
   - Comfort Mode: Include settings to reduce motion sicknesses, like vignettes or blinkers.

4. **Comfort Settings:**
   - Tunnel Vision: Offer the option to enable a tunnel vision effect during movement.
   - Gameplay Customization: Difficulty Levels: Provide multiple difficulty settings for different player skill levels.
   - Game Speed: Allow users to adjust the game's pacing.
   - AI Behavior: Enable users to modify the behavior of in-game AI or enemies.

5. **Customization:**
   - Avatar Customization: Offer options for users to customize their avatars.

- Home Environment: Allow users to personalize their in-game home or hub.
- Content Level Customization: Supernatural[72] is a VR game that offers players customized fitness programs ranging from beginner to advanced levels, catering to various skill sets across different content.

6. **Social Settings:**
   - **Friend List:** Implement a friend system to foster social interactions in the game, complete with badges and real-time status updates to indicate friends' online presence, thereby promoting multiplayer engagement and social connectivity.
   - **Personal Space vs. Shared Space:** Provide users with the ability to designate private and shared spaces within the application. For instance, in Vision Pro, users have the option to configure which windows are for public view and which are kept private.

7. **Preferences and Save Data:**
   - **Auto-Save Frequency:** Allow users to set how often the game auto-saves.
   - **Data Management:** Provide options for data backup and deletion.

Accessibility Settings:

- **Colorblind Modes:** Implement various color schemes for colorblind users.
- **Subtitle Options:** Enable subtitles with customization for font size and color for different languages.
- **One-Handed Mode:** "Implement One-Handed Mode for users with limited mobility, including those with a single hand or facing challenges like disabilities or medical conditions.

---

[72] Supernatural, https://www.getsupernatural.com, accessed Jan. 2024

○ **Height:** Provide the user with options to adjust their height settings or choose between sitting and standing positions based on their current posture.

Building Blocks for Personalization

Components:	Actions:
Audio Settings	• Volume Controls • Audio Effects • Voice Chat
Enhanced Aesthetics	• Clean and uncluttered designs
Control Customization	• Button Mapping • Field of View (FOV) • Dominant Hand • Sensitivity
Movement Options	• Options of movements • Comfort Mode
Accessibility Settings	• Colorblind Modes • Subtitle Options • One-Handed Mode • Height
VR Comfort Settings	• Tunnel Vision • Gameplay Customization • Game Speed • AI Behavior
Customization	• Avatar Customization • Home Environment

Content Level Customization	• Beginner to Advanced • Content Variations
Social Settings	• Friends System • Personal Space vs. Shared Space
Preferences and Save Data	• Auto-Save Frequency • Data Management
User Profiling and Data Analysis	• Using User's data to customize the needs (Vision Pro)
Contextual-Awareness Design	• Adaptable UI and Objects that Understand the environment
AI Assistant	• Personalized the needs through conversation
Avatar Personalization	• Let users create their own style of avatar(s)
Inclusivity	• Include the experience design with Dyslexia, low vision… and more.

Evaluate

"If you cannot measure it, you cannot improve it."
-Lord Kelvin

Key Design Patterns:

1. **Feedback:** Create a good single interactive element for each interaction such as audio, haptics, visual cues, smell, and voice response. Feedback can also serve as guidance in immersive apps.

2. **Performance:** An individual's evaluation of a complex task forms the basis for enhancement and refinement such as performance, scores, and data.

3. **Data-Driven Assessment:** Follow the data. Go with what works. Data is systematically collected and analyzed to inform and improve educational practices, policies, learning outcomes, and monetization strategies.

4. **AI Evaluation and Automation:** Integrate Generative AI into both online and offline systems to minimize friction based on AI assessments.

Why is Evaluation important?

For fitness apps and training simulations in fields like medicine, evaluation is vital for gauging performance and making improvements. For example, in fitness XR apps, users receive data on calories burned and their leaderboard ranking, offering tangible measures of their workout's effectiveness. Similarly, feedback in spatial design, job simulations, and medical training is crucial for honing skills and enhancing precision and accuracy. This highlights the broader principle that without measurable feedback, it's challenging to assess and improve performance in any field, whether it's for productivity, fitness, or professional training.

What is Evaluation?

The definition of Evaluation is *"the process of judging or calculating the quality, importance, amount, or value of something."*[73] It guides the refinement of user experiences and technological advancements.

There are 2 methods for evaluation:

1. **Feedback:** A single reaction to an object or UI when being triggered. (simple reaction)

2. **Performance:** An individual's assessment of a task, which serves as a foundation for improvement. (Complicated tasks)

Visual, Auditory, and Haptic Feedback

Navigating user experiences in virtual spaces can be challenging. Designers often aim for users to engage with tutorials sequentially, yet users may become sidetracked by exploring other features or elements not central to the intended path. Unlike traditional 2D media like films and video games, where a camera guides the audience, virtual environments lack this directional control. Thus, employing visual, audio, and haptic cues is crucial to guide users toward the next segment of the narrative.

These cues act as "Signifiers" to help users comprehend the next step. Feedback plays a pivotal role in enhancing the spatial computing experience. Integrating haptics, force feedback, tactile sensations, audio, and visual cues seamlessly can greatly enhance the user's sense of presence and immersion. These elements help create a deeper connection between the user and the virtual environment, elevating their overall engagement.

---

[73] Cambridge Dictionary, https://dictionary.cambridge.org/us/dictionary/english/evaluation, accessed Jan. 2024.

It's important to understand how feedback can be effectively utilized. In the VR game "The Line," users are not merely observers but active participants. Their interactions with various handles drive the narrative, immersing them deeply in the story. Every interaction will trigger feedback (storytelling). The Line is an experience where the player is a crucial part of the unfolding narrative. After delving into the immersive 360-degree VR 3D cinema, players gain the power to make significant decisions or actions, like pulling a crucial lever, which in turn shapes the story's progression.

Providing immediate visual or auditory feedback for actions helps users understand the consequences of their actions, reducing the likelihood of errors. For example, a confirmation sound or visual cue when an item is selected or placed can be very effective. In the game "Cubism," a feedback sound is triggered when a player inserts an incorrect shape.

In the context of user experience, Beat Saber, a popular VR game, serves as an excellent illustration of the effective integration of haptics, audio, and visual cues. When players engage with the game, these sensory cues are skillfully employed to provide comprehensive feedback. During gameplay, as the player wields their virtual lightsabers to slice through oncoming targets, haptic feedback in the form of controller vibrations aligns with the physical impact, creating a tangible sense of interaction. Audio cues, such as a satisfying slicing sound, accompany each successful hit, enhancing the auditory dimension of feedback. The visual component further elevates the experience by displaying on-screen indicators of whether targets are accurately struck or missed.

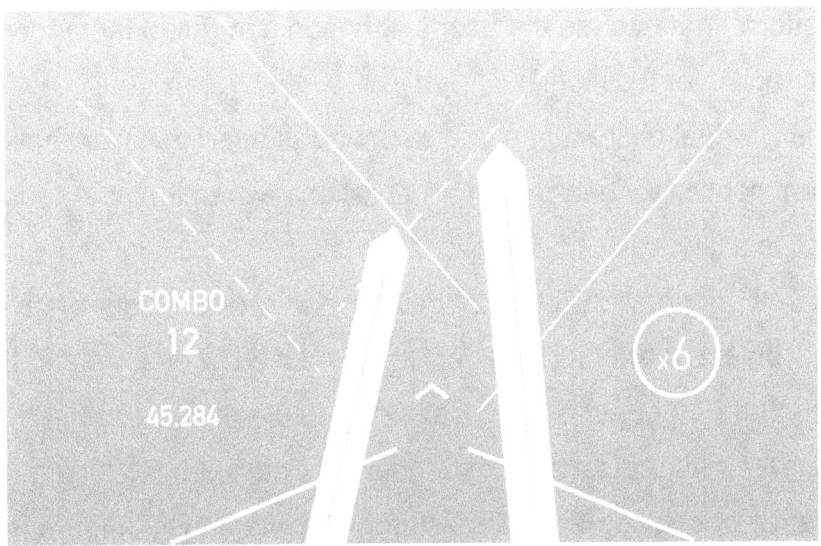

Fig. 3.77: Beat Saber: Haptics + Audio + Vision Cues. The player knows how many combos he/she hits, and scores numbers immediately.

Moreover, Beat Saber utilizes voice instructions during onboarding, ensuring that players receive clear and immersive guidance, while text cues on the path provide additional visual reinforcement. This holistic approach to leveraging haptics, audio, and visual cues exemplifies the seamless integration of sensory feedback for an engaging and instructive experience.

Feedback as Guidance in Immersive Apps

In immersive applications, users can sometimes find themselves at a standstill, unable to discern the next step in their journey. To mitigate this, feedback can be effectively used as a subtle hint, guiding them forward. By implementing a time threshold, hints or feedback can be provided to ensure continual engagement with the app.

Effective methods for crafting such hints include:

- Dim ambient lights and spotlighting specific objects or areas to draw attention.
- Outline objects when users interact, either through gaze or physical interaction.
- Create a glowing effect where particles highlight scenes or objects of interest.

- Sound effects that capture the user's attention and guide them towards a particular action or location.
- Introduce a virtual character to interact with the user, to direct their focus.
- Implement haptic feedback, such as vibrations, when the user touches or approaches a key area.
- Gaze-based Triggers: Utilize gaze detection to provide hints when a user looks at a specific object or area for a certain amount of time, offering just-in-time guidance that's triggered by the user's own exploratory behavior.
- Adaptive Difficulty: Adjust the frequency and detail of hints based on the user's performance or choices. For users struggling with a task, offer more detailed guidance, while for those excelling, keep hints minimal to maintain challenge.
- Voice Commands and Feedback: Incorporate voice interaction to allow users to request help verbally and receive auditory hints, making the experience more interactive and accessible, especially in situations where visual cues might clutter the interface.
- Non-Linear Hint Systems: Design hint systems that allow users to access hints on demand in a non-linear fashion, enabling them to seek help for specific challenges without being forced through a predetermined path of learning.
- Personalized Learning Paths: Analyze user data to offer personalized hints that cater to individual learning styles and preferences, enhancing the effectiveness of guidance provided.

These techniques not only enhance user experience but also ensure a smoother, more intuitive interaction within the immersive environment.

Performance

One of the successful features is the assessment each time right after the user finishes the task. The user can understand their performance immediately and get motivation to perform better next time.

If you're looking to explore and experiment with diverse hand-physics mechanics for your upcoming application, there's an excellent resource readily available. You can easily access the "Hand Physics Lab" application from the Meta Quest Store. This app provides an invaluable opportunity to delve into the realm of hand gesture control and discover the myriad possibilities it offers. You can gain hands-on experience with various hand-physics mechanics, helping you better understand how these mechanics can be harnessed to enhance user interactions in your project.

Many fitness apps, job simulations, medical training, and games have a lot of assessments to measure your performance. It can be a combination of skill sets or a series of feedback to accumulate assessment.

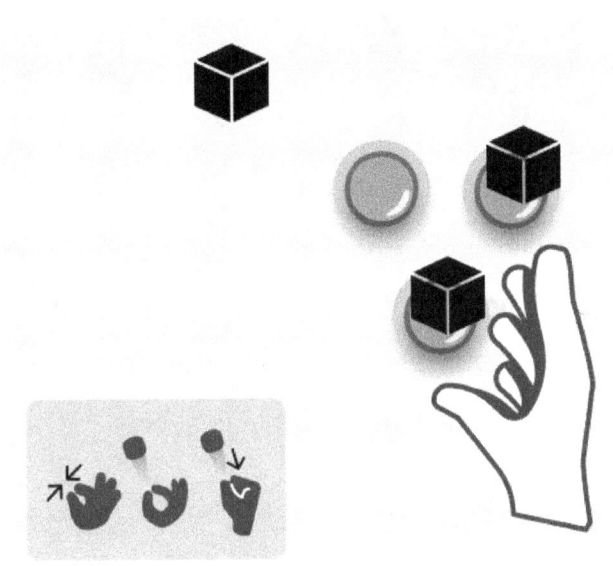

Fig. 3.78: Hand Physics Lab developed a series of assessments designed to evaluate the accuracy of hand-tracking technology. These tests enable users to interact with virtual objects and receive real-time feedback on their manipulation. The assessments focus on demonstrating how effectively a user's hand movements are translated into actions within a digital environment, allowing for a tangible understanding of the technology's precision and responsiveness.

Les Mills Body Combat VR melds fitness with virtual reality, bringing the acclaimed Les Mills martial arts workouts into an exhilarating VR challenge. Whether you're a martial arts buff or seeking a unique fitness experience, this game offers a thrilling dive into virtual combat fitness.

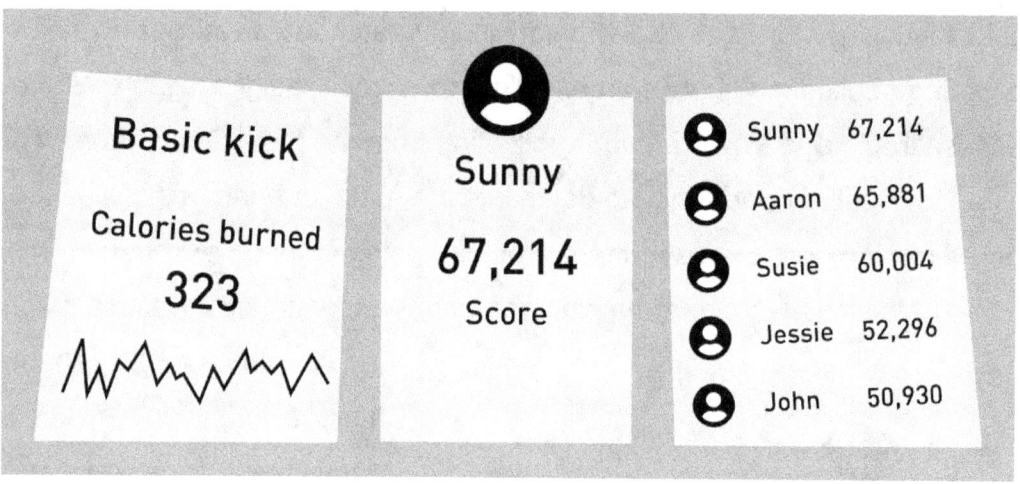

Fig. 3.79: Les Mills Body Combat has a leaderboard with all the results for each session. It helps the player understand how he/she performs during the session.

After each exercise, you'll receive feedback on your performance and see your ranking among friends, further motivating players. Fundamentally, feedback, onboarding, and hints are pivotal in determining whether users are captivated by or alienated from the spatial computing experience.

AI Evaluation and Automation

Many warehouses and retail companies, including Walmart, are leveraging computer vision technology to optimize inventory management in their warehouses. Walmart's upcoming "Walmart InHome Replenishment" initiative, a part of its subscription based InHome delivery service, aims to streamline the online shopping experience by automatically filling shopping carts with frequently purchased items.

At CES 2024 in Las Vegas, Walmart CEO Doug McMillon, in collaboration with Microsoft CEO Satya Nadella, highlighted the potential impact of Generative AI in grocery shopping. The keynote emphasized the development of an AI-powered automated replenishment system within Walmart's InHome Delivery program. This system, tailored to analyze and learn from individual shopping and consumption habits, is designed to autonomously replenish goods, eliminating the need for physical store visits. Available through the Walmart+ InHome service, which began in 2019 and includes delivery options to a customer's door, garage, or refrigerator, this innovative system adjusts based on a customer's unique purchasing patterns. The initiative was inspired by customer insights indicating the burdensome nature of regular household shopping and planning.

Data-Driven Assessment

"Turn VR games into a game that improves brain health." -Amir Bozorgzadeh

Gamification can help to increase user engagement and help the user enter a flow state. Amir Bozorgzadeh, CEO of Virtuleap, has previously used VR to treat acrophobia and believes that the 2D screen experience serves merely as an introduction to the more immersive VR or spatial experience. For effective data generation and problem-solving, he advocates for a full-body immersive environment, utilizing comprehensive tracking systems. Amir highlights the potential of AI algorithms in gathering extensive data from VR experiences to uncover insights into cognitive abilities and challenges. He points out that VR's true power lies in its data collection and analysis capabilities, which can significantly contribute to understanding conditions like ADHD and autism, and in fostering the integration of neurodiverse individuals into the workforce. Virtuleap also collaborates with Roche, and MIT to gather more research data, aiming to improve treatments for conditions like ADHD and Alzheimer's.

Virtuleap gamified health care by developing Enhance VR, a VR app available on the Quest Store, in which neuroscientists take the lead as product owners. They use their expertise to design games, which are then developed in collaboration with Unity game developers, starting from a Game Design Document (GDD) to prototyping and user testing/feedback stages. Enhance VR offers daily brain training sessions with a variety of short, engaging, and challenging games designed by neuroscientists. These games are tailored to improve a range of cognitive skills such as memory, attention, flexibility, problem-solving, motor control, spatial orientation, and information processing. The focus is on minimizing the entertainment aspect of the games to reduce their addictiveness. Amir's goal is not to create a game that users become addicted to;

rather, he wants to enhance VR to serve as a tool for measurement and cognitive improvement, avoiding the pitfalls of addiction.

Building Blocks for Feedback

Components:	Actions:
Feeback	• Create a good single interactive element for each interaction such as audio, haptics, visual cues, smell, and voice response.
Performance	• An individual's evaluation of a complex task forms the basis for enhancement and refinement such as performance, scores, and data.
AI Evaluation and Automation	• Integrate Generative AI into both online and offline systems to minimize frictions based on AI assessments.
Draw attention	• Dim ambient lights • Spotlight effect • Sound effects • Introduce a virtual character to interact with the user • Haptic feedback

Gaze or physical interaction	• Outline objects when users interact
Request help	• Voice Commands
Personalized Learning Paths	• Analyze user data to offer personalized hints

Safe

"Precaution is better than cure."
–Edward Coke

Key Design Patterns:

1. **Physical Safety:** Spatial computing experiences can be immersive, often making users less aware of their physical surroundings. Ensuring physical safety means preventing accidents and injuries that could occur from collisions with real-world objects, falls, or strain due to extended use.

2. **Psychological Safety:** The immersive nature of spatial computing can also impact mental health. Content that is too intense, realistic, or disturbing can cause psychological distress. Protecting users from such content and ensuring they can easily exit an experience is vital.

3. **Privacy Protection:** Protect user data by developing clear privacy policies that inform users about how their data is used and stored. And only get the data that is required for the experience.

4. **Secure Architecture:** Design an infrastructure with security as a priority. Regular security audits and updates can help safeguard against data breaches and unauthorized access.

5. **Social Interaction:** Spatial computing platforms often include social components where users interact with others. Ensuring these interactions are safe and respectful is important to prevent harassment, bullying, and other forms of abuse.

6. **Ethical Considerations:** As spatial computing technologies can be used to create highly realistic simulations, there are ethical implications around consent, manipulation, and the distinction between reality and virtual experiences.

7. **Data Encryption & Data Layers:** Implementing end-to-end encryption for any data transmitted by devices, including visual, auditory, and biometric data, to

protect user privacy. Use multiple data layers that include public records of private properties and restricted areas to accurately map out game-safe zones.

8. **Anonymous Avatars:** Allowing users to interact in virtual environments using avatars that do not disclose their real identity to ensure privacy.

9. **Minimal Data Retention:** Platforms can adopt policies of collecting the minimum necessary data for operation and regularly purging unnecessary user data to protect privacy.

10. **Consent for Data Collection:** Transparent policies and user consent protocols for any personal data collection, with clear options for users to opt out of data collection in spatial design applications.

11. **Secure Account Management**: Features like two-factor authentication, parental controls, and the ability to review and manage connected devices help prevent unauthorized account access and protect user identities.

12. **Data Privacy Controls:** Offering robust user control over what data is shared and who can see their activity, profiles, or presence in an environment.

13. **Community Reporting:** Integrate a feature that allows the community to report unsafe or inappropriate locations. The game developers can then modify these areas or remove them from the game. Clearly inform players about the importance of respecting private property and not trespassing. This could be included in the game's terms of service, tutorial, or periodic reminders within the game itself. Provide real-time warnings or alerts in the game if a player is approaching a private or restricted area. Establish a clear code of conduct that outlines acceptable and unacceptable behaviors within the VR environment. Make sure all users agree to these terms before participating.

14. **Auditing and Compliance:** Regular audits of platforms to ensure they comply with international privacy regulations like GDPR or CCPA, reassuring users that their data is handled responsibly.

15. **Parental Control:** Empower parents to regulate both the duration and content of their children's virtual reality engagement. With Meta Parental Control, parent-supervised accounts have been crafted specifically for Meta Quest 2 and Meta Quest 3 users in the preteen group of 10-12 year-olds. These specialized accounts allow preteens to explore a carefully selected range of age-appropriate apps and experiences from Meta's expansive VR catalog. Featuring sophisticated parental control options, stringent data privacy protocols, and detailed management and oversight functions, these accounts enable parents to create a secure and manageable VR environment for their young ones.

Why is Safety Important?

Historically, certain AR games have been criticized for inadvertently leading players to trespass on private property, sparking significant safety and privacy issues. Similarly, in virtual meeting spaces, instances of uninvited participants, known as "Zoombombing," have compromised the security of platforms, resulting in confidentiality breaches. Additionally, several VR platforms have grappled with harassment incidents within their virtual environments, highlighting the urgent need for improved moderation tools to ensure user safety in social settings. Moreover, the practice of utilizing eye-tracking and biometric data in VR for targeted advertising has prompted serious concerns regarding user consent and the ethical handling of personal data for advertising profiling.

Safety plays a vital role in the adoption of spatial design products, where extensive personal data is often required for features like room and iris scanning, movement and speech recognition, and behavior analysis. The collection of such sensitive information necessitates robust user trust, especially as privacy concerns grow. In spatial design, ensuring user safety and privacy becomes paramount, as simulations often expose a user's surroundings and personal details. The protection of data such as facial recognition, names, addresses, and family information is crucial, as this data can potentially be accessed or shared by companies, governments, or advertisers for profit.

Thus, the success of spatial design products relies on the ability to guarantee data security and user privacy.

In the book, *"Your Face Belongs to Us: A Secretive Startup's Quest to End Privacy as We Know It,"* Kashmir Hill investigates the alarming rise of facial recognition technology, focusing on the controversial firm Clearview AI. As a New York Times tech journalist, she critically examines Clearview's app, capable of identifying individuals from a single photo and revealing their online presence, including personal and social details.

What is Safety?

In the evolving digital realm, we are witnessing a transformation that is reshaping our experiences. This digital shift, whether embraced or not, carries significant implications. Challenges present in the real world are likely to be magnified in digital and immersive spaces. For instance, harassment, which is already a concern within 2D online environments, could become tenfold more impactful in a fully immersive digital world. Therefore, it's crucial to prioritize privacy, safety, and actively promote DEI (Diversity, Equity, and Inclusion) principles during the development of spatial design technologies to ensure a safe and inclusive digital future.

Safety in XR and spatial computing platforms is multifaceted, encompassing physical safety to prevent accidents due to immersion, psychological safety to protect mental health from intense content, data privacy, and security to safeguard sensitive information from theft or surveillance, cybersecurity to defend against hacking and cyber-attacks, social safety to ensure respectful interactions and prevent abuse, accessibility to include users of all abilities, and ethical considerations to manage the realistic simulations and their effects on users. Each aspect is vital to creating a secure, respectful, and inclusive environment for all users.

Physical Safety

Guardian Systems

VR systems like Meta Quest have "Guardian Systems" that allow users to define their play area and create virtual boundaries that appear when users get too close to the real-world limits, preventing physical accidents. As for AR mobile games, implement geofencing to prevent the game from placing objectives or items of interest within private properties or sensitive locations. Geofencing uses GPS to create a virtual boundary around a particular geographical area.

Fig. 3.80: Guardian Boundary Play Area

A Personal Boundary

In Meta Horizon Worlds, it functions as a safeguard for your avatar's personal space in the virtual environment. When an individual approaches too closely, the system automatically stops them at the edge of this boundary, with no physical sensation or haptic feedback to the user. This feature enhances previous measures against hand harassment, which made an avatar's hands vanish when they entered another's personal space.[74]

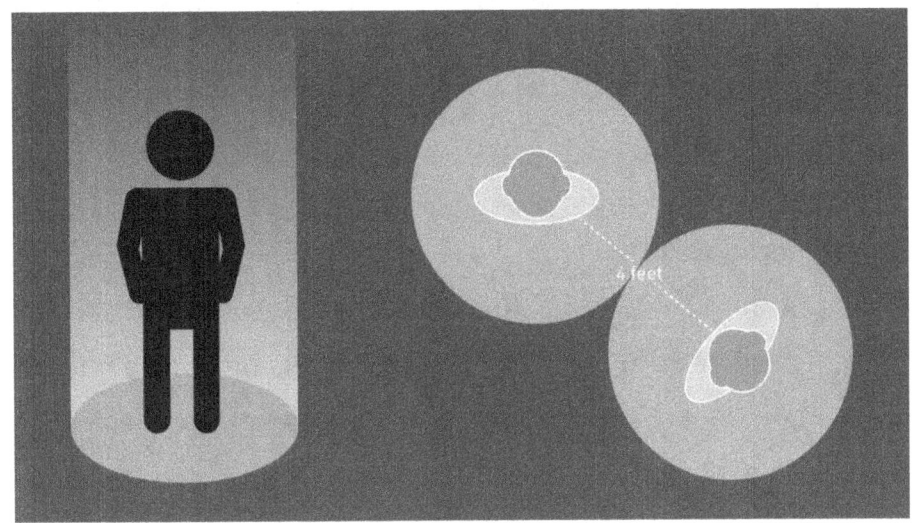

Fig. 3.81: A Personal Boundary sets a perimeter around your avatar, ensuring that no one can encroach upon your character's personal space.

Potential Risk of Passthrough Devices

Ori Inbar highlighted the significant risks associated with using passthrough devices in high-risk environments, such as working on wind turbines. These devices, which display the real world through cameras, can pose serious hazards if they fail. In such an event, the user could be rendered effectively blind in a perilous situation.

In contrast, see-through devices, which allow users to directly view the real world, are deemed safer for industrial use. In the event of a failure, the impact is comparable to wearing a pair of sunglasses, thus presenting a lesser risk. The industry anticipates the emergence of AR glasses that can seamlessly integrate AR content with the real world, blurring the line between virtual and actual elements. However, deploying these advanced technologies in high-risk environments, such as industrial workplaces, will be challenging due to the necessity of maintaining constant awareness of the real surroundings. There's a clear distinction in the application of AR and VR technologies between industrial and consumer contexts. In industrial settings, the emphasis is on

---

[74] Meta, https://about.fb.com/news/2022/02/personal-boundary-horizon, accessed Jan 2024.

safety and uninterrupted perception of the real world, favoring the use of see-through devices. Conversely, in consumer applications where safety concerns are less critical, pass-through devices are more suitable. These offer benefits such as a wider field of vision and enhanced rendering capabilities.

Psychological Safety

Harassment & Cyberbullying

In some metaverses and VR platforms, harassment cases, particularly targeting women and young teens, have been reported. The immersive and embodied nature of virtual reality intensifies the impact of such experiences, making harassment feel more realistic and traumatic. This is attributed to the direct connection between a person's physical body and their avatar, potentially leading to mental health issues and trauma. A woman, recounting her harassment experience on one such platform, described being so shocked that she couldn't remember how to use the controller to exit, likening the experience to a nightmare.

To combat virtual harassment in XR or metaverse environments, a multi-faceted approach is essential. Platforms must implement and enforce robust community guidelines alongside effective reporting systems. These could include AI monitoring or intuitive emergency triggers like iris detection or physical reaction sensors, acting like an 'airbag' for immediate protection. Establishing a proper emergency system necessitates a diverse creation and engineering team (DEI) in terms of race, gender, and age. Currently, male-dominated teams may overlook or deprioritize harassment issues due to a lack of empathy with the victims' situations. Incorporating more diversity into these teams is vital to ensure the safety and well-being of all users in virtual environments.

Cybersecurity

To prevent cyber-attacks in XR platforms and spatial computing, a comprehensive security approach is vital. This includes robust authentication and access controls, data encryption, regular software updates, and network security measures like firewalls and intrusion detection systems. Secure application development practices, strong privacy protections, user education, and an effective incident response plan are also crucial. Continuous system monitoring for anomalies and collaborative information sharing about emerging threats and best practices among security professionals further fortify these platforms against cyber-attacks. Staying abreast of the evolving cybersecurity landscape is essential for maintaining robust defenses in these advanced technological environments.

We Have Less and Less Privacy

"Eyes are the window to the soul, mind, and body." -Damon Hernandez

Vision Pro's "Optic ID" integrates an eye-hand interface for device unlocking, ensuring high security as the data is encrypted and stored within the device's Secure Enclave processor, making it inaccessible to Apple or third parties. This technology, utilizing a unique Iris ID for everyone, is increasingly prevalent across various sectors for its precision and security. While it enhances operational efficiency in areas like border control, banking, and healthcare, and offers a secure alternative to traditional access methods in high-security environments, it raises privacy concerns. The unique biometric nature of iris scans could potentially expose personal and emotional information, leading to privacy risks and potential for emotional manipulation, highlighting the need for careful consideration of privacy and personal autonomy in the implementation of this technology.

Damon Hernandez, CEO and Co-Founder of Mixx Reality raised ethical concerns regarding iris scanning for biometric identification, including the potential for companies to exploit individuals' iris data for commercial purposes. It also touched upon the medical applications of iris scanning, such as early disease detection. The technology can also predict the excitement and reactions of the users. He addressed that we might need to initiate ethical conversations surrounding these technologies, especially considering their potential long-term implications as soon as possible.

Learn and Participate from Existing Standards

Metaverse Standards Forum is a venue for standard organizations to coordinate help with Metaverse safety and privacy issues. The mission of the Metaverse Standards Forum aims to encourage and enable the timely development of open interoperability standards essential to an open and inclusive Metaverse.

The Metaverse Standards Forum plays a crucial role in enhancing safety and privacy in the Metaverse. The Forum's approach includes pragmatic, action-based projects like implementation prototyping, hackathons, and plugfests, and they work on developing consistent terminology and deployment guidelines. This collaboration helps coordinate requirements and resources to foster the creation and evolution of standards within relevant domains.

X Reality Safety Intelligence (XRSI) is a nonprofit organization focused on ensuring safety, privacy, security, inclusion, and responsible innovation in emerging technologies. It establishes baseline standards and addresses challenges in these domains through a global network of researchers, advisors, and experts. XRSI's work spans various initiatives, including the development of a Privacy and Safety Framework and supporting efforts like the Child Safety Initiative and Medical XRSI. They aim to build trust and promote safe and inclusive environments within the field of emerging technologies.

The XR Guild is a non-profit collective of Spatial Computing professionals, dedicated to instilling ethical practices within emerging technologies like AI and XR. They emphasize the absence of established ethical frameworks in these fields, despite their transformative potential. Recognizing the dual nature of these technologies—offering both promise and peril—the XR Guild calls for a cultural shift toward ethics in the industry. They stress the importance of every professional, from designers to developers and researchers, taking responsibility for ethical considerations and learning from past mistakes. By fostering this ethical culture, they aim to ensure that XR and AI advancements benefit humanity positively. Individuals and companies are invited to support their mission by signing their letter.

The Open AR Cloud Association (OARC) also views the Metaverse Standards Forum as a vital component in promoting open standards, interoperability, privacy, and security for a real-world Metaverse or Spatial Web. These examples showcase how the Metaverse Standards Forum and its collaborating organizations are striving to address safety and privacy concerns, ensuring a secure and user-friendly Metaverse experience.

Trust is Earned: Data Self Sovereignty

Before collecting data, it is crucial for companies and developers to inform users about how their data will be used, addressing this issue transparently. Terry xR. Schussler highlighted that "Trust is earned, not given!" particularly relevant in designing spatial experiences and handling user data. It's crucial to clearly communicate what data exchange entails. Consider the software industry 20 years ago: software was sold in large boxes containing disks and manuals, with a notice on the box stating, "By opening this software box, you have already agreed to the terms." Terry pointed out the absurdity of expecting users to agree to unknown terms before even opening the box. Nowadays, due to past incidents of data leaks, people have become more conscious about their data. For instance, before collecting data, users might see a popup explaining, "We designed the Passthrough API with privacy in mind. Apps using this API cannot access, view, or store images or videos from the device sensors. This ensures on-device processing of raw sensor data." This way, users comprehend the necessity of their data and its intended use, fostering trust and transparency.

Another approach is Self-sovereign identity (SSI),[75] a digital identity model that empowers individuals with complete control over their personal information. This model

---

[75] Wiki, Self-sovereign identity (SSI) is an approach to digital identity that gives individuals control over the information they use to prove who they are to websites, services, and applications across the web.

allows users to manage and present their identity to websites, services, and applications across the web, ensuring they maintain full control of their data.

Design, Security, and Privacy

In spatial design and development, the substantial amount of user data accessed by developers poses a risk. Developers must ensure they request only essential data from users and store it securely. This data can include account and device information, inferred approximate location from IP addresses, social connections for multiplayer features, app analytics activity data, and access to microphones or cameras for interactive experiences. Additionally, apps may collect sensitive data such as health metrics, room dimensions, emotional behavior, iris IDs, etc.

Companies like Meta require developers to adhere to privacy laws, maintain transparent privacy policies, and obtain user consent for data use. Within the Meta ecosystem, payment information is exclusively managed by Meta, preventing developers from directly accessing this sensitive data. Users retain the right to manage their data, including the ability to review and modify privacy settings in environments like Meta Quest.

For Apple's spatial computing platforms, the company's commitment to user data security is evident in its App Store Review Guidelines. Apple prioritizes a safe user experience, with a thorough review process for all apps to prevent data misuse or intellectual property violations, leading to strict consequences for non-compliance. Apple mandates developers to implement robust security measures for proper user data handling and to prevent unauthorized access or disclosure. Furthermore, Apple insists on explicit user consent and clear notification during activities that involve recording or logging user activity, including the usage of device cameras, microphones, and screen recordings.

Damon Hernandez highlighted the crucial role of spatial designers in addressing key issues like trust, privacy, data protection, and safety, especially given the varied permission levels for data access. While convenient, managing this data responsibly is vital. He delved into integrating immersive technologies in the real world, with a focus on mixed reality gaming and IoT applications. He underscored their potential impact on design and user experience, including developing tools for mixed reality content. Particularly noteworthy was his work on interactive 3D profiles for stakeholders in a Helsinki building project, emphasizing customizing information according to user needs and permissions, accessible at different levels to the public, building owners, and investors. Furthermore, Damon discussed the promising yet challenging role of digital twins in property management, highlighting the potential security and privacy risks posed by big companies with access to vast data, who may not be adept at safeguarding it. He underscored the importance of non-profit organizations like XR Guild in raising ethical issues and protecting rights to prevent technology from spiraling out of control.

Building Blocks for Safety

Components:	Actions:
Guardian + Boundary Systems	• Create Guardian and Avatar Personal Boundary
Robust Community Guidelines	• A Clear, strict, and well-enforced community guidelines
Effective Reporting Systems	• Quick report system
Blocking and Muting Features	• Ability to block or mute other users
Personal Space Settings	• A Personal space bubble
Educating Users	• Educate users through tutorials, reminders, or hints.

Moderation	• Human moderators or AI tools
Anonymity Controls	• Requiring a verified user account
Collaboration with Law Enforcement	• Protocols for collaborating with law enforcement
Community Building and Positive Incentives	• Encourage positive behavior through rewards or recognition systems
Research and Feedback	• Gathering users' feedback to improve
Design, Security, and Privacy	• Request only essential data from users and store it securely
Privacy Protection	• Protect user data by developing clear privacy policies that inform users about how their data is used and stored.
Learn and Participate from Existing Standards	• Learn from Metaverse Standards Forum, X Reality Safety Intelligence (XRSI), The XR Guild, and The Open AR Cloud Association (OARC)
Trust is Earned: Data Self Sovereignty	• Before collecting data, it is crucial for companies and developers to inform users about how their data will be used, addressing this issue transparently. • Self-sovereign identity (SSI), a digital identity model that empowers individuals with complete control over their personal information.

Conclusion

"Stay hungry, stay foolish."
-Steve Jobs

In this chapter, we delved into ten core principles of spatial design. Yet, the secret to exceptional experience design transcends merely understanding these principles; it involves creatively diverging from them. Experimentation plays a crucial role, as does conducting user testing in real-world scenarios to collect market feedback. This approach is fundamental for gaining deeper insights into spatial experience design.

These principles serve as the initial framework at the dawn of spatial design, yet the field is in a state of rapid evolution, propelled by technological advancements and yielding continual discoveries. The most impactful design principles often depend on market trends and user preferences. Current user preferences are likely to shape the design standards of tomorrow. Spatial design, being an emergent field, presents a vast expanse for these principles to morph, adapt, and mature. Furthermore, valuable lessons can be learned from the official resources of headset manufacturers like Vision Pro, Meta Quest, HTC's app store, and Hololens, among others. These sources provide broad guidelines that are continually refined through user feedback and optimization. Thus, maintaining a perpetual cycle of learning from users, embracing emerging technologies, engaging in active experimentation, and staying adaptable to change is crucial for crafting compelling experiences in the era of spatial design.

4

Tools and Pipelines

Designers in spatial design have access to an array of platforms and tools, encompassing 2D/3D art creation software, rapid prototyping tools, game development engines, WebXR development tools, development kits, virtual worlds, and MMO (Massively Multiplayer Online) platforms. These resources empower designers to push the boundaries of creativity and innovation in the spatial domain.

Spatial Design Devices

The VR and AR industry is advancing rapidly with devices like Meta Quest 3, HTC Vive XR Elite, Pico 4, Magic Leap 2, XReal Air 2, HoloLens 2, and Varjo offering immersive experiences. These devices feature high-resolution displays, advanced tracking technologies, and varying degrees of integration with virtual and physical realities. Apple Vision Pro joins this lineup with mixed reality capabilities. Additionally, Android and iOS devices support AR features, with Android offering a range of AR-compatible smartphones and iOS devices leveraging high-quality cameras and ARKit for spatial computing. Each device caters to different user needs, from entertainment to professional applications. Here is a breakdown of the leading devices:

Apple's Vision Pro

Apple's Vision Pro headset employs a distinctive system known as visionOS to craft an immersive experience. Unity has launched PolySpatial[76] as a dedicated development

---

[76] Unity PolySpatial, https://docs.unity3d.com/Packages/com.unity.polyspatial.visionos@0.1/manual/index.html, accessed Feb. 2024.

tool for visionOS. Applications and games developed in Unity can natively function on Apple Vision Pro, leveraging innovative visionOS features such as swift pass-through and high-definition graphics rendering.

Vision Pro delivers an exceptional visual experience in a lightweight headset, featuring a resolution exceeding 4K for each eye. This device is engineered for spatial computing, meaning it integrates seamlessly with the real world. Embracing a more natural user interface (NUI), eliminates the need for traditional controllers, instead utilizing eye tracking, hand gestures, and voice commands for environmental interaction.

With Vision Pro, there is no need for a guardian or set boundary. Users can employ the digital crown to determine the level of immersion desired. Adjusting the digital crown allows for a flawless fusion of digital content with one's physical surroundings. For co-location and multi-user interactions, Apple employs photorealistic avatars to symbolize users cohabiting in a shared environment. In this communal space, all participants can view the content, while a private space acts as a control panel, visible solely to the individual user. Sectors such as medical, automobile, architecture, and B2B training will likely see advancement with the release of Vision Pro.

Apple has released Ferret, an advanced multimodal AI model, as open source, showcasing its capabilities in interpreting conversations about images through the integration of visual and textual data analysis. This initiative underscores Apple's unexpected dedication to open-source AI projects and heralds a new era of innovation in intelligent multimodal systems. As a result, spatial computing is set to become the cornerstone for AI technologies that will streamline everyday tasks in the foreseeable future.

Meta Quest 3

The Meta Quest 3 stands out as a cutting-edge Mixed Reality (MR) headset, boasting 4K resolution LCD screens and streamlined pancake lenses. Powered by the Snapdragon XR2 Gen 2 processor, it delivers exceptional graphics quality. The headset is outfitted with advanced sensors and cameras, enabling rich MR experiences. Featuring the innovative "Touch Plus" controllers, equipped with infrared and internal sensors for precise user interactions and powered by AA batteries, the Quest 3 signifies a significant leap in merging virtual and physical worlds.

It offers immersive experiences through hand-tracking, eye-tracking, voice commands, and sophisticated passthrough, along with comprehensive room understanding and depth-sensing technologies. Continuing the Meta Quest tradition, it provides high-quality, accessible VR experiences with built-in tracking, an extensive library of games and applications, and the convenience of wireless operation. Each new model in the Meta Quest series seeks to surpass its predecessors by enhancing resolution, processing power, battery life, and comfort, as well as broadening features for gaming, socializing, and productivity.

HTC Vive XR Elite

The HTC Vive XR Elite, unveiled at CES 2023, is a versatile mixed reality (MR) headset that seamlessly combines the digital and physical worlds. It boasts a high-resolution passthrough for depth-sensing accuracy, and diopter adjustments for crisp visuals, alongside a stunning 3840x1920 screen resolution. Designed for convenience, it features detachable batteries enhancing its portability, supports seamless wireless PC VR gaming, and provides detailed hand tracking at the skeletal level. The headset integrates with VIVERSE for a range of activities and is compatible with the VIVE Ultimate Tracker for precise body and object tracking. It also comes with the VIVE MR Gasket, ensuring maximum comfort and spatial awareness. Compact, lightweight, and built for both gaming and professional use, the Vive XR Elite stands out with its high-resolution display, broad field of view, powerful processing, and comprehensive tracking capabilities. It represents HTC's latest stride in immersive technology, designed to appeal to both enthusiasts and professionals seeking high-quality MR experiences.

Pico 4

Developed by ByteDance, the Pico 4 VR headset targets the virtual reality gaming market, available in Europe and East Asia but not in the United States. Featuring pancake lenses and dual LCD displays for enhanced resolution and lightweight design, it offers real-time hand tracking and passthrough mode. As a standalone device, it competes in the consumer VR space with a focus on comfort, high-resolution visuals, a broad field of view, advanced tracking for precise interaction, and versatility for both gaming and non-gaming applications.

Magic Leap 2

The Magic Leap 2 is an ergonomic, lightweight AR headset tailored for enterprise, featuring a 70° field of view, dynamic dimming, high-resolution optics, and runs on a 7nm AMD quad-core processor with 16GB RAM and 256GB storage. It supports multiple input methods, including a precision controller, hand, and eye-tracking, and offers advanced spatial audio. Focused on data privacy and cloud autonomy, it operates on Magic Leap OS, aiming to boost enterprise productivity, collaboration, and 3D visualization through immersive technology, marking a significant advancement in bridging digital and physical workspaces.

XREAL

The XREAL Air 2 glasses are an augmented reality solution noted for improved design, offering a brighter, lighter, and more comfortable experience. It features high-resolution Sony Micro-LED displays, a wide field of view, and a 120FPS refresh rate, ensuring crisp and clear visuals. Compatible with various devices including iPhone 15 models and most Android flagships via a USB-C port, these glasses also come with built-in speakers and a set of useful accessories. Despite some issues with compatibility and fit, as well as a basic style without additional add-ons, the XREAL Air 2, is praised for its excellent image quality and ease of use, making it a significant step forward in the AR glasses market.

Hololens 2

Developed by Microsoft, the HoloLens 2 is a mixed reality headset launched in 2019, designed to enhance efficiency and accuracy across industries such as construction, healthcare, education, and manufacturing. It boasts an ergonomic design, a 52-degree field of view, and advanced holographic processing including eye and hand tracking. Aimed at enterprise use, it supports applications like training, remote assistance, and 3D visualization to boost productivity and collaboration, making it a pivotal tool for transforming work processes and educational outcomes through immersive technology.

Varjo

Varjo stands out in the high-end VR and MR headset market, focusing on professional use. Their products, such as the Varjo XR-4 series, are celebrated for photorealistic fidelity, closely mirroring natural vision. Widely applied in astronaut training, automotive design, and medical research, Varjo's headsets merge immersive experience with high-resolution displays, supporting diverse professional needs. The company is committed to revolutionizing industry workflows through its pioneering technology, offering unmatched visual precision crucial for simulation, training, and research.

Android devices

Several Android device models support augmented reality (AR) features. Some popular models include the Google Pixel series, Samsung Galaxy S series, OnePlus smartphones, Huawei Mate series, and many others. Additionally, many newer Android devices are equipped with the necessary hardware and software to support AR applications. For the most accurate and up-to-date information, it's best to check the official specifications or documentation provided by the manufacturer of a specific Android device.

iOS Devices

Apple has been advancing spatial computing on iOS devices (iPhone 6S and up), particularly iPhones and iPads, through key features like high-quality cameras for augmented reality (AR), the ARKit framework for developing AR applications, and the integration of LiDAR scanners in newer models for precise environment mapping. These capabilities are combined with seamless integration within the Apple ecosystem, enhancing the overall AR experience on iOS devices. For detailed and up-to-date information, it's best to consult Apple's official resources and announcements.

Spatial Design Tools

Here is a list of development tools for spatial design, encompassing 2D/3D design enhanced by GenAI technology, art preparation, and various prototype and development platforms:

2D/3D Art Creations

Figma stands out for UI design and team brainstorming, while Adobe Illustrator and Photoshop are essential for advanced 2D art. Blender, enhanced by AI plugins like Stable Diffusion, offers a full spectrum from 3D modeling to game creation, backed by extensive community support. Maya is crucial for AAA game assets, 3ds Max for realistic environments, and Cinema 4D for VFX and motion graphics. ZBrush excels in 3D sculpting and character design. Innovative AI tools such as Blockadelabs, Meshy, and Anything World are transforming asset creation, streamlining design processes.

Rapid Prototype Tools

Creators aiming for quick prototyping and team collaboration, without the need for mastering complex tools, may find the artist/designer standard pipeline most fitting. ShapesXR, which is widely used by numerous universities and enterprises, stands as the go-to platform for rapid collaboration and ideation. This tool is particularly effective when used with a Meta Quest headset, enabling immersive collaboration where creators can design experiences directly in their visual field. For those who do not have access to a Head-Mounted Display (HMD) like Meta Quest, or who prefer a more traditional web 2D platform for prototype, Bezi offers an alternative solution. Bezi is a webXR tool designed for rapid prototyping and collaborative efforts, requiring only a laptop and a web browser. This versatility makes it accessible to a broader range of users, ensuring that collaborative design work is possible regardless of the hardware requirement.

SentioVR is designed for professionals in architecture, engineering, and construction, offering VR design reviews and interactive 3D presentations. It's compatible with SketchUp, Revit, and Meta Quest headsets, featuring VR conversion of panoramas, interactive tours, and remote VR meetings. Arkio facilitates spatial design on VR, desktop, and mobile platforms. It supports fast modeling, cross-platform collaboration, and workflow integration with Revit, Rhino, and Unity, allowing intuitive shape manipulation and mixed-reality experiences. Gravity Sketch, a 3D design software, enables designers to create in 3D from the start using VR tools. It supports real-time collaboration across VR, iPad, and desktop platforms, and includes LandingPad for cloud-based content access.

Game Engine & Platforms

Unity is favored for spatial design due to its cross-platform capabilities, extensive toolset for immersive creation, ease of use, and ability to manage 2D and 3D content. Its asset store and large community offer valuable resources and support. Unity frequently updates to incorporate the latest tech advancements. In the realm of XR and spatial computing, Unity provides a robust framework for developing VR, AR, and mixed reality applications, supporting the full development cycle from design to deployment, thus enabling the creation of spatially interactive content for various devices.

The Unreal Engine development pipeline is tailored for spatial design using OpenXR, offering optimized, high-quality rendering for complex scenes. It features robust support for evolving ecosystems, enables cross-platform deployment, and is designed for performance optimization across devices. Additionally, it supports customization and extensibility through Blueprint scripting or C++ coding and provides a wealth of resources including templates, samples, and a comprehensive asset library to aid developers in creating immersive spatial design experiences.

XCode for visionOS/Vision Pro

Xcode is Apple's integrated development environment (IDE) for creating applications across various Apple platforms. With support for macOS, iOS, iPadOS, watchOS, tvOS, and visionOS, developers utilize Xcode to build, test, and debug their applications. For Apple's Vision Pro headset, developers are expected to leverage Xcode for tailored spatial computing applications. The headset's standalone functionality and connectivity to Mac present opportunities for seamless app experiences, emphasizing spatial computing with features like motion gestures, eye tracking, and speech recognition. Integration of ARKit and SceneKit frameworks within Xcode could further enhance the creation of augmented reality experiences for the Apple Vision Pro.

METAVRSE - Web-Based XR Platform

METAVRSE[77] is a web-based platform for creating 3D interactive experiences, compatible with various devices. It features a powerful 3D engine for diverse applications like training and e-commerce and supports all major operating systems and browsers. As one of the leading platforms in spatial computing and 3D content creation, METAVRSE is recognized by partnerships with Microsoft and Epic MegaGrants and is a member of the Metaverse Standards Forum.

---

[77] METAVRSE, https://metavrse.com, accessed Jan. 2024.

Development Kits

The Meta Quest XR SDK[78] is tailored for spatial design experiences on Meta Quest headsets, offering features like passthrough support for blending the virtual and real worlds, plane detection for context-aware experiences, and device tracking for accurate placement of virtual content. Microsoft's MRTK is an open-source kit for mixed reality applications across platforms, enhancing development with 3D interaction models and UI controls. ARKit and ARCore, for iOS and Android respectively, are frameworks for building AR experiences, leveraging device capabilities for motion tracking and environmental understanding. Vuforia, a versatile AR SDK, excels in tracking and image recognition, enabling interactive AR applications for mobile devices and digital eyewear. Each toolkit caters to different aspects of spatial design, from specific headset functionalities to broad mobile AR capabilities.

Mobile & Social Media

Lens Studio, developed by Snap Inc., is a user-friendly platform enabling the creation of AR experiences for Snapchat. It offers tools for crafting AR lenses, filters, and effects, incorporating 3D objects, animations, and interactive elements. The platform supports both novice and experienced developers, featuring face tracking, hand tracking, and machine learning capabilities for enhanced AR immersion.

SparkAR, by Meta, provides users with a versatile augmented reality platform for crafting interactive experiences across Facebook, Instagram, and Messenger. Offering tools for building AR filters, effects, and animations, SparkAR supports features such as face tracking, hand tracking, and object recognition, catering to a broad audience from casual users to experienced developers.

---

[78] Meta Quest XR SDK, https://developer.oculus.com/documentation/unity/unity-gs-overview/,accessed Jan. 2024.

WebXR

WebXR development encompasses various stages, ranging from conceptualization and design to deployment. Creators initiate the experience by ideating and selecting tools such as WebXR APIs and frameworks like A-Frame, Babylon.js, and 3D libraries such as Three.js. They then craft optimized multimedia assets. The development phase involves coding with HTML, JavaScript, and WebXR APIs, with testing, debugging, and optimization ensuring compatibility and optimal performance.

8th Wall is a platform that empowers developers to build augmented reality (AR) applications that can run on a variety of devices, including smartphones and tablets. Known for its WebAR capabilities, 8th Wall enables the creation of AR experiences that can be accessed through web browsers without the need for additional apps. The platform supports features like surface tracking, image recognition, and hand tracking, allowing developers to create interactive and dynamic AR content. It is designed to be versatile, offering compatibility with both iOS and Android devices.

Virtual World and MMO Platforms

Numerous options, such as Horizon Worlds, VRChat, Roblox, Fortnite, and Minecraft, offer virtual world creation with massive multiplayer online (MMO) capabilities. Features like character creation, environment building, and community development are common across these platforms. For business training, options like Engage VR, Spatial, and Mozilla Hubs are available. These user-friendly virtual MMO platforms allow creators to build on existing platforms, leveraging established user bases, but customization may be limited, requiring adherence to platform rules or payment of fees for benefits.

Alex Fernandez, Co-Founder and Chief Product Officer at Nspire, highlighted the effectiveness of Horizon Worlds in reducing the friction typically associated with creating social VR experiences. He praised its powerful creation tools, which facilitate collaboration and real-time brainstorming using tangible materials. Horizon Worlds is portrayed as an all-encompassing platform, ideal for learning, team formation, brainstorming, and assembling a game. It offers both no-code and code-based options, making it a versatile prototype tool for diverse creative needs.

The Creation Pipelines

Ideations

When approaching ideation, one effective method is to immerse yourself in a spatial environment and begin creating using tools such as ShapesXR. Alternatively, if you favor traditional techniques, you might start by sketching your ideas on paper and then moving on to prototyping. You can also employ various materials like cardboard or Lego, or even explore through acting and filming. However, before delving into these hands-on tools, it's advisable to consult the Unity Game Design Document (GDD).[79] Although primarily aimed at game development, I've discovered that the Unity GDD is extremely useful for spatial design planning. There are different ways to realize creative ideas, including using ShapesXR for spatial ideations and employing 2D sketching, storyboarding, and acting for more traditional conceptualization methods.

Spatial Ideations (Product/Project-Based) -

ShapesXR

"Every time I come up with a new concept, I immediately put on my headset and launch ShapesXR. There, I create some simple props and frames to experiment with my idea, seeing if it's feasible or not. Once I have something tangible, I quickly bring in stakeholders to provide real-time feedback on the development." - John Hanacek, XR Designer at Nanome Inc.

---

[79] Unity GDD, https://connect-prd-cdn.unity.com/20201215/83f3733d-3146-42de-8a69-f461d6662eb1/Game-Design-Document-Template.pdf, accessed Jan. 2024

John Hanacek and Inga Petryaevskaya (CEO of ShapesXR), address the evolving needs in XR design by using spatial prototype - ideation and collaboration in virtual space. John advocates for a purpose-driven approach, utilizing tools like ShapesXR to delve into XR's capabilities and to design with intent. He sees XR as a medium for "external imagination," crucial for creating shared visual experiences and fostering collaboration.

Inga mentioned that it's important to acknowledge the limitations of tools like Figma for 3D XR design. While Figma excels in 2D brainstorming and 2D UI design, it falls short in facilitating collaboration in a 3D space. In immersive environments, comprehending scale, distance, and tangible experiences is crucial. Conceptualizing a fully immersive space through a 2D screen is challenging, as it doesn't allow for iterative exploration of scale, ergonomics, and 360-degree surroundings. The difference between using hands to create tangible elements versus imagining a 3D space with a 2D screen and mouse is significant. For ideating immersive spaces, employing a 3D immersive approach is more effective than using 2D tools to visualize a 3D environment. Shapes 2.0 is a potential game-changer for UX and UI in XR. She acknowledges the power of Blender but warns of its complexity - creating 3D objects in 2D space requires a lot of mouse-hand-brain coordination with the imagination of how it might look in 3D space through a 2D screen, advocating for Shapes' efficiency in rapid prototyping.

Both John and Inga highlighted the shift from traditional 2D planning to immersive 3D creation, underscoring the need for tools that accommodate quick iteration and ease the design process for both individual creators and collaborative teams.

Sketching, Storyboarding, and Acting

If you prefer the 2D way for planning and love using the 2D way of thinking - easy, fast, no headset required, here are some ways for you for 2D ideations.

- **Templates for AR/VR Sketches:** Volodymyr Kurbatov, a Product Designer specializing in AI, VR, and AR, is the innovative mind behind Inborn Experience.

He has developed a set of templates designed to assist in the iterative planning of hand, controller, and environment aspects within the 3D setup. Kurbatov has identified key limitations in traditional 2D UX planning, such as the absence of considerations for scale, rotation, distance, and the first-person point of view. With his groundbreaking 3D spatial architecture-like sketch templates, designers and creators can now strategically plan and envision projects in the dynamic realm of 3D space.[80]

Fortunately, implementing specific techniques enables efficient idea iteration and content development, fostering collaboration among diverse team members and disciplines. The **Microsoft Mixed Reality Design Training**[81] page suggests 3 immersive ways of quickly brainstorming: Bodystorming, Acting, and Storyboarding.

Bodystorming   **Acting**   **Storyboarding**

Fig. 4.1: Bodystorming, acting, and storyboarding (Resource: Microsoft)

Bodystorming: Bodystorming is a quick, hands-on prototyping method for testing interactions, digital objects, UI, and animations using crafting materials. It allows design teams to experiment with proposed features and mechanics without extensive prototyping. The aim is to gather actionable input, receive testing feedback, and spatially conceptualize.

---

[80] Templates for AR/VR Sketches, https://medium.com/inborn-experience/templates-for-ar-vr-sketches-e424dfb60e54, accessed Jan. 2024
[81] Microsoft Mixed Reality Design Training page, https://learn.microsoft.com/en-us/training/modules/intro-to-mixed-reality/6-design-3d, accessed Jan. 2024.

Acting: Act out user movements in your mixed reality experience. This testing phase involves exploring ideas in three-dimensional space and getting feedback, particularly beneficial for non-technical team members or stakeholders. For instance, acting out a mixed reality hospital experience to a medical professional can yield valuable insights.

Storyboarding: Selecting the optimal method to communicate your ideas and proposed experience depends on the target audience. For presenting ideas to a development team, bodystorming and acting out the experience. However, when aiming to persuade stakeholders or non-technical team members, opting for high-fidelity assets like storyboarding may be more effective.

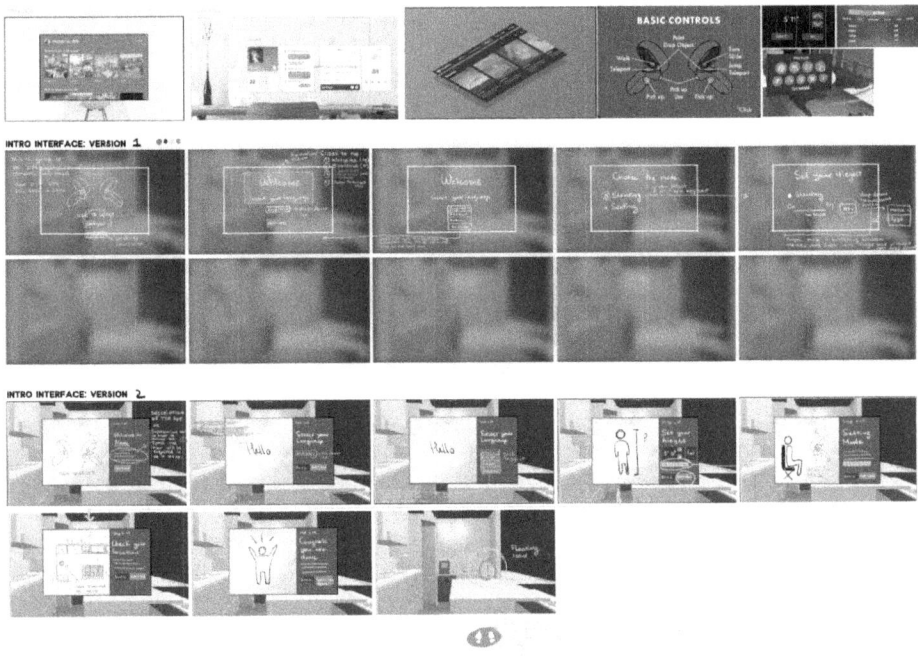

Fig. 4.2: Storyboard by Kateryna Bielotserkovska, VR/AR Unity Developer (Resource: Kateryna Bielotserkovska)

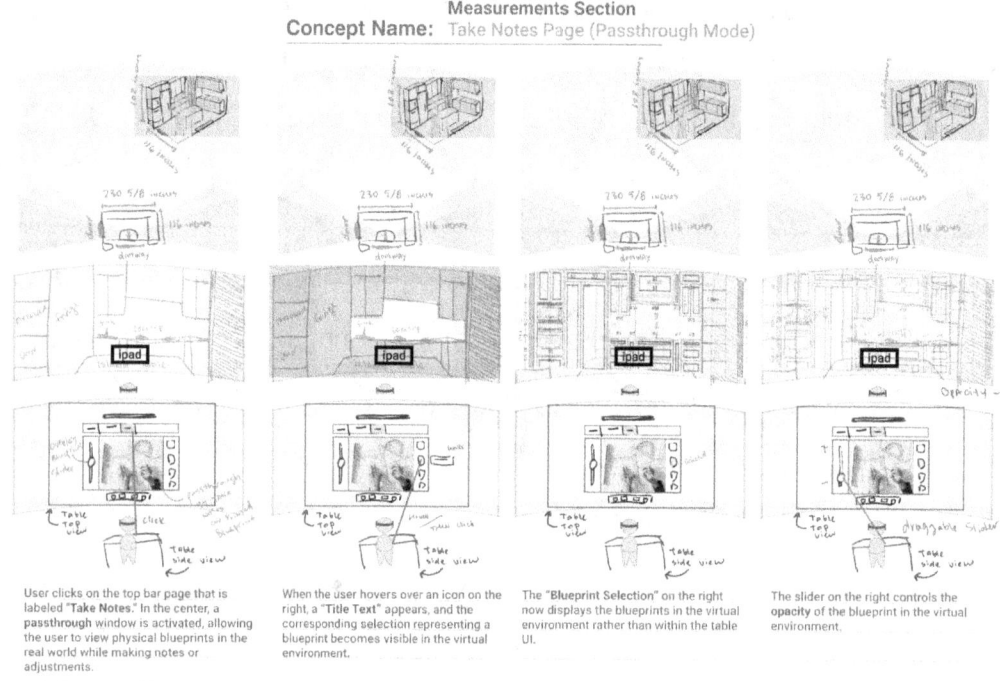

User clicks on the top bar page that is labeled "**Take Notes.**" In the center, a **passthrough** window is activated, allowing the user to view physical blueprints in the real world while making notes or adjustments.

When the user hovers over an icon on the right, a "**Title Text**" appears, and the corresponding selection representing a blueprint becomes visible in the virtual environment.

The "**Blueprint Selection**" on the right now displays the blueprints in the virtual environment rather than within the table UI.

The slider on the right controls the **opacity** of the blueprint in the virtual environment.

Fig. 4.3: UI in 3D Space and Interaction Storyboard by Kateryna Bielotserkovska, VR/AR Unity Developer (Resource: Kateryna Bielotserkovska)

Getting User's Feedback and Keep Improving

Put Yourself in the User's Shoes: Remember, we're all human. Your experiences and comforts often mirror those of others. To understand this better, immerse yourself in the experience by using a headset or device. Notice your reactions - do you feel dizzy or comfortable? As a first-time user, assess how intuitive it is to interact with objects in the scene. Do you enjoy the experience? If not, consider what improvements can be made. In the words of Sam Hessenauer, CTO at Nanome, users in an immersive environment expect a highly polished experience. A barebones or unfinished application can significantly detract from user comfort, especially in an immersive setting. For instance, a poorly designed cube interaction might be passable on a 2D screen but can cause cognitive and physical discomfort in an immersive mode. Always aim for an experience that is not only functional but also comfortable and engaging for the user.

Production Pipelines

Standard Development Pipeline - Unity

Development in Unity requires an understanding of coding, 3D modeling, and design/art skills, along with powerful PC and spatial design headsets/devices. It's ideal for developers, designers, and business professionals with coding abilities or those interested in learning to code. Unity's popularity in spatial design stems from its cross-platform compatibility, vast community support, and abundant educational resources. Its SDK support extends across multiple platforms, including desktops (Windows, Mac, UWP, Linux), mobile (iOS, Android), spatial design systems (ARKit, ARCore, HoloLens, etc.), consoles (PlayStation, Xbox, Nintendo Switch, Google Stadia), and web and embedded systems (WebGL, Embedded Linux, QNX).

About Unity

Unity is a widely recognized game engine and development platform known for its versatility and user-friendly interface. It is extensively used by game developers, artists, and designers for creating both 2D and 3D games, as well as interactive experiences. In the field of spatial design, Unity is notable for its multiplatform support, enabling the deployment of games and applications across a variety of platforms, including mobile devices, PCs, consoles, and spatial design systems. The platform offers a comprehensive set of features for graphics, physics, and animation, and includes tools for real-time collaboration and an extensive asset store. Unity supports several programming languages, most prominently C#, providing a versatile environment for developers of varying skill levels.

In the area of AI, Unity offers tools for game development and real-time 3D experiences. Unity Muse facilitates rapid development using simple text prompts and advanced AI technologies. Unity Sentis allows for the integration of AI models into the Unity Runtime, enhancing the capabilities of games and applications on user devices. The Unity Asset Store offers a selection of AI-driven solutions and assets for game development. Additionally, Unity demonstrates its AI capabilities with Orb, an AI-driven character dynamically created on the user's device, showcasing the potential of AI in character development and real-time interaction.

For development, access to current tutorials is essential. Unity has substantial community support and provides free, high-quality educational materials on its website and YouTube, catering to a broad range of learners.

Workflow for Unity Pipeline

1. **Select the Unity Version and Template:** Install relevant SDKs through Unity (like ARCore, ARKit, Meta SDK, MRTK, OpenXR… etc.). Then select a template such as 2D, 3D, Universal Render Pipeline, VR, or AR.

2. **Asset Creation:** Import assets such as 3D models (Blender), animations, audio, and textures. For the 2D UI assets, normally it was exported from Figma. Unity can create very basic 2D and 3D assets on its native platform, but it has very limited functions. Or you can go to Unity Asset Store[82] to purchase assets for build. For 3D models creation, normally you can use Blender to create and use Stable Diffusion AI to generate/map the texture. Unity also uses Unity Sentis which allows you to import your own AI model. Unity Muse allows creators to use text prompts to create. Those tools accelerate the building process.

3. **Programming:** Then you can start building the logic and structure for your development. Write scripts for gameplay, interactions, physics, and other functionalities using C#. Integrate features like hand tracking, gaze control, etc.

4. **Testing and Iteration:** For testing, you can upload the Unity package to your device platform to get testing links for your Beta users, or you can bring your PC and native build to share with your users to do in-person testing.

---

[82] Unity Asset Store, https://assetstore.unity.com, accessed Jan. 2024.

5. **Iterative Development:** Regularly update the project based on feedback and testing results, refining features, and fixing bugs.

6. **Optimization:** Optimize for the best performance on target devices, focusing on frame rates, memory usage, and battery life.

7. **Accessibility:** Ensure that the spatial design experience is accessible to a diverse range of users.

8. **Deployment:** Build and Packaging: Prepare final builds for the target platforms (like iOS, Android, PC VR, etc.).

9. **Distribution:** Deploy the application on platforms like the Meta Store, SteamVR, HTC, Apple App Store, Google Play, or enterprise solutions.

Standard Design Prototype Pipeline - ShapesXR

ShapesXR is an innovative tool built for spatial app design whether it is a VR, AR or Mixed Reality game, app, or experience, streamlining collaboration in virtual spaces for rapid, collective decision-making. It enhances the social aspect of virtual collaborations with 3D avatars and allows for real-time adjustments, fostering a more interactive experience. The platform's unique "holonotes" feature supports spatial feedback, facilitating asynchronous communication. In VR, ShapesXR excels at 3D manipulation, offering users the ability to interact directly with objects and check designs in real time. It includes functionalities for 3D sketching, and storyboarding, and integrates seamlessly with external workflows like Unity. This makes ShapesXR particularly adept at quickly setting up 3D scenes, prototyping, and brainstorming within spatial design environments. As a comprehensive prototyping tool, ShapesXR offers an array of features including 3D creation, collaborative design, compatibility with various formats, interactive prototyping, and mixed-reality integration. It's tailored to simplify development processes from the conceptual stage to the final presentation, proving invaluable for teams in the industry.

Here's the ShapesXR pipeline:

1. **Headset Compatible:** So far ShapesXR is compatible with Quest 2, Pro and 3, Pico 4. Go and download ShapesXR from the Meta Quest Store and Pico Store.

2. **Create a ShapesXR account:** Follow the instructions to pair your headset and set up your account on your ShapesXR 2D desktop app for future shared room and project management.

Fig. 4.4: Pair up your headset and create an account on your ShapesXR desktop app. (Source: ShapesXR)

3. **Jump in and Start Creating:** After you finish creating an account, put on your headset and go to the lobby to pick a space and start to create. For ShapesXR, it has a lot of great tools to start. You can go to *Learn ShapesXR*[83] to learn more about how it works. ShapesXR offers comprehensive and intuitive tools for 3D creation. Users can start with simple brushstrokes or use the extensive library of primitives, modifying colors and materials, adding text, and assembling complex designs and scenes. The platform's precise snapping system aids in creating detailed and accurate spatial designs.

Here are the features you can access through controllers:

---

[83] Learn ShapesXR, https://learn.shapesxr.com, accessed Jan. 2024.

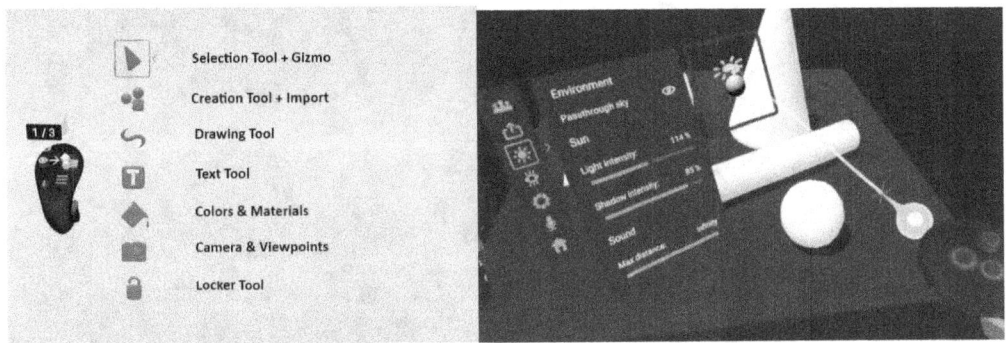

Fig. 4.5: In ShapesXR, the users use the controller interface to quickly access the creation tools. (Source: ShapesXR)

4. **Import and Export Compatibility:** The platform supports a variety of 2D UI assets from Figma and 3D formats like JPG, PNG, OBJ, GLB, and glTF. It also integrates with Figma frames and components through a plugin, keeping assets synchronized. Users can import and manage assets via a web app and, upon completion, export them as glTF or directly to Unity, making it versatile for various development pipelines.

5. **Collaboration-Focused Design:** ShapesXR, crafted for creative brainstorming and teamwork, enables simultaneous co-creation in both VR and mixed-reality.

6. **(Passthrough) Settings:** By entering a simple space code, team members can access a communal virtual space, enabling them to brainstorm and evaluate designs as if they were in the same physical location. This feature greatly enhances their spatial comprehension of the project. Specialists from diverse disciplines can participate, dynamically iterating and visualizing their concepts in 3D. This approach promotes efficient idea synchronization and communication across the team.

Fig. 4.6: In ShapesXR, it allows creators to collaborate and present the concept. (Source: ShapesXR)

7. **Prototyping and Presentation:** ShapesXR empowers users to transform their designs into interactive prototypes, presentations, and storyboards. Its intuitive 'Stages' system facilitates the creation of captivating and engaging prototypes. This feature enables users to simulate interactions, allowing for rapid prototyping without the need for coding. Users can easily invite others to test ideas or present them to stakeholders, offering a dynamic and immersive experience for showcasing concepts. The 'Stages' functionality not only simplifies the prototyping process but also enhances team presentations and feedback sessions. The "Interactivity" feature in VR prototypes also aids in showcasing a product's or experience's potential to stakeholders or investors, offering a more concrete and immersive representation of the concept.

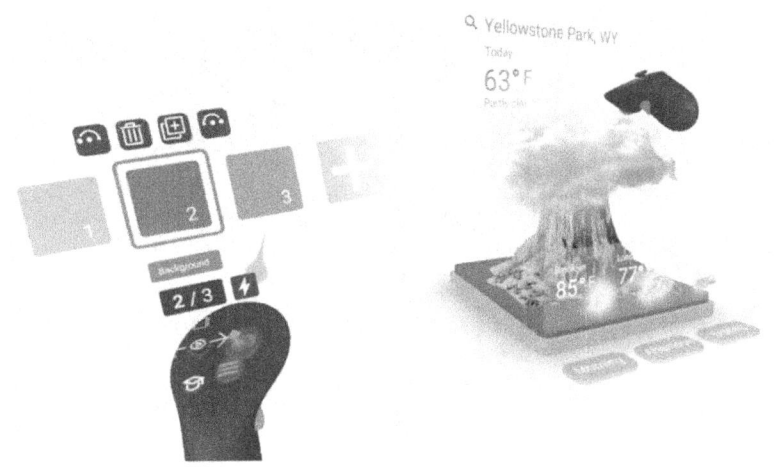

Fig. 4.7: In ShapesXR, "Stages" enables users to simulate interactions, allowing for rapid prototyping without the need for coding.

Fig. 4.8: ShapesXR also allows for the addition of interactive elements to enhance presentations. Currently, it includes functionalities such as "On click," "On hover enter," "On hover exit," and "After delay." These features enable dynamic engagement within the showcased content. (Source: ShapesXR)

8. **Mixed Reality Features:** The platform crosses virtual boundaries with its Mixed Reality features. Users can add passthrough materials to emulate occlusion, and more, effectively bridging the gap between digital content and the physical environment. This feature is particularly useful for bringing digital designs into a real-world context.

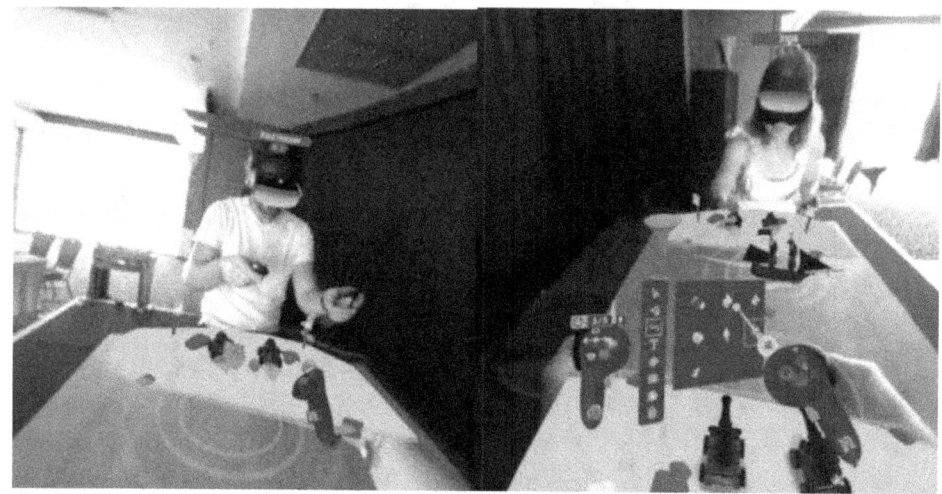

Fig. 4.9: In ShapesXR, it allows users to prototype in Mixed Reality. (Source: ShapesXR)

9. **Import to Unity:** You can also import the ShapesXR file to Unity to export to the app. Once you export into Unity, you can pretty much export to any device compatible apps including Meta Quest apps, WebXR and Vision Pro.

MMO Platform Pipeline - Horizon Worlds

Alex Fernandez, Co-Founder and Chief Product Officer of Nspire, underscored the significance of shared spaces for collaborations in spatial design. He stressed that physical co-presence greatly enhances collaboration and brainstorming, streamlining the journey from conceptualization to production. This highlights the crucial role of direct engagement and collective creativity in the design process. Alex pointed out that Horizon Worlds delivers a holistic experience, spanning from initial idea generation and prototyping to publishing games and experiences on its platform.

This mirrors the capabilities of platforms like Roblox, which provides creator tools, and Fortnite, utilizing the Unreal Engine Fortnite (UEFN). These platforms offer an array of resources and tools, enabling users to craft their own games beginning with pre-made templates and frameworks. This method significantly expedites development, allowing creators to avoid the laborious process of starting from zero. Beyond easing the transition from ideation and collaboration to final release, these platforms also aid in cultivating a community around the created content.

Currently, Horizon Worlds does not have a direct monetization route for individual creators. However, there are opportunities for revenue generation for established teams or organizations through designing and building worlds for larger entities, with the potential for charging for these specialized world-building services.

Pipeline Overview:

1. **Team Collaboration:** Utilize Horizon Worlds for team collaboration. The platform's user-friendly tools facilitate quick adaptation and use.

2. **Asset Creation:** Employ various tools like Blender, Maya, and Unity for asset creation. Horizon Worlds features "Local Scripting," akin to visual scripting, enabling users to craft interactive elements within the platform.

3. **Publication and Iteration**: Launch the creation on Horizon Worlds, gather user feedback, and continually iterate based on this input.

Cross-Platform Design Pipeline - Bezi

Cecilia Uhr, Co-Founder of Bezi, introduced the company's vision to establish a cross-platform tool for XR designers to showcase their ideas. Reflecting on her experiences at Meta, she expressed frustration with the limitations of using Unity for prototyping. Her goal was to develop a tool that accelerates the prototyping process for product designers. To achieve this, Bezi's team drew inspiration from familiar design platforms like Figma and Blender, ensuring the interface remains intuitive for designers accustomed to these tools.

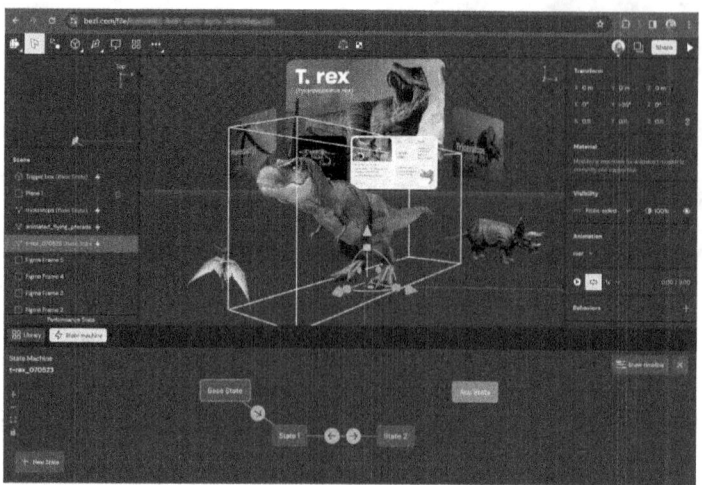

Fig. 4.10: Bezi's team has skillfully incorporated elements from well-established design platforms such as Figma and Blender.

A standout feature of Bezi is its web-based 2D platform, eliminating the need for a headset and allowing immediate work on prototypes. Bezi incorporates a state machine and visual scripting to facilitate the rapid creation and sharing of prototypes. Sharing is as simple as sending a URL, and prototypes can be accessed on various devices if there's an internet connection.

Fig. 4.11: Bezi stands out with its web-based 2D platform, which removes the necessity for a headset and enables instant development of prototypes.

Bezi Pipeline:

1. **Figma to Bezi:** Import your 2D designs into Bezi.

2. **Bezi Platform:** This web-based platform lets design teams collaborate on a 2D screen. Designers can craft interactions and animations using state machines and visual scripting. The web-based nature of Bezi means prototypes are easily shared through URL links.

3. **Bezi to Unity:** Prototypes from Bezi can be imported into Unity, allowing them to be exported to Unity-compatible platforms, ranging from devices like Meta Quest to WebXR.

Fig. 4.12: Prototypes created in Bezi can be seamlessly imported into Unity, facilitating their export to a variety of Unity-compatible platforms.

WebXR Development Pipeline

The WebXR application allows for experiences with variable input controls. Typical browsers that support WebXR include Google Chrome, Mozilla Firefox, Microsoft Edge, Oculus Browser, and Samsung Internet Browser. While Safari has shown limited or experimental support, it's important to note that the extent of WebXR features and performance can vary across these browsers. Compatibility also depends on the hardware, such as VR headsets or XR-capable devices. Browser support for WebXR is an evolving field, so staying updated with the latest versions and capabilities is recommended.

WebXR Pipeline:

- **Tool and Platform Selection:** You can use WebGL in Unity by installing a WebXR Exporter package[84] or using WebXR APIs, 3D modeling software, web development frameworks like A-Frame, or Babylon.js.

- **Asset Creation:** You can create 3D models and import them to the web or use Three.js for 3D models, textures, animations, and other multimedia content to be created. These assets need to be optimized for web performance to ensure smooth loading and rendering.

- **Development and Coding:** Using HTML, JavaScript, and WebXR APIs, developers write the code to bring the experience to life. This involves implementing interactions, physics, and the integration of 3D assets. As for no no-code solution, Mozilla Hubs and Frame VR are good tools for creating a WebXR multiplayer platform. Frame VR is user-friendly, offering no-coding creation tools, a developer API for customization, and a supportive community. Key features include multi-user interaction with avatars, voice, and text, as well as tools like webcams, screen sharing, whiteboards, and polls. Administrators can set permissions, passwords, and user roles, and the platform supports collaborative building.

- **Optimization:** Performance is key in webXR, so this stage involves optimizing the experience for different devices, improving loading times, and ensuring a smooth, high-quality experience.

- **Deployment:** Once the application is ready, it's deployed on a web server. WebXR experiences are typically accessible through a URL, making them easy to share and access on compatible devices.

---

[84] WebXR Exporter package, https://assetstore.unity.com/packages/tools/integration/webxr-exporter-109152, accessed Jan. 2024

- **Maintenance and Updates:** Post-launch, the spatial design experience might need updates for new content, bug fixes, or performance improvements. Continuous monitoring and maintenance are essential.

- **User Feedback and Iteration:** Collecting user feedback and monitoring how users interact with the experience can provide valuable insights for future improvements and updates.

Vision Pro Spatial Computing Pipeline

As for the Vision Pro development pipeline, here are 2 major ways to do it. One is from XCode, and the other one is from Unity PolySpatial development.

1. **XCode (SwiftUI)** - Since it is Apple's native platform, you can customize it easily. Download XCode and use SwiftUI and Reality Composer Pro for 3D creation. Since it is using Entity Component System (ECS), all the UI visual representation requires coding. And for the 3D manipulation, it uses a USDZ file. You can use Reality Composer Pro to change the size, add different simulations for it, and use ARKit in visionOS API if you want to have full-body and hand-tracking experience. If you want to create an immersive experience, use Metal for immersive apps.

2. **Unity PolySpatial**: Developers can use PolySpatial to port existing virtual reality experiences or create new ones, mix content with passthrough for immersive experiences that blend digital content with the real world, and run multiple immersive applications side by side in passthrough within the Shared Space.

Conclusions

"The only way to do great work is to love what you do."
– Steve Jobs

Spatial design is transforming across numerous industries through AI and innovative technologies, allowing for a diverse selection of tools and devices tailored to various creative preferences. From initial ideation to final realization, spatial design's immersive storytelling environments span from traditional 2D platforms to advanced headset development, accommodating both no-code and coding approaches. If your goal is to focus on creative concepts, no-code tools offer simplicity and efficiency. However, for those aiming to develop a unique IP platform that can generate profit and scale up, coding becomes a crucial skill. Choose the path that aligns with your objectives and leverages the vast possibilities within spatial design to achieve your vision.

5

What's Next?

Now we are entering an era in which AI helps accelerate all areas of content creation and software development. In this chapter, I've summarized the advice of 38 XR & spatial computing industry leaders for people who are interested in breaking into this field:

1. **Job vs. Career**
2. **How to Break into Industry?**
3. **AI Took Our Jobs vs. Integrate AI**
4. **Technology Convergence in Industries**
5. **To Code or Not to Code**

Job versus Career

In the past, the path to success seemed linear: attend a reputable school, secure a well-paying job, continuously hone your skills, and gradually ascend to higher-paying positions. This trajectory was a common pursuit.

However, the landscape began to shift dramatically during the COVID-19 pandemic from 2020 to 2022. Students increasingly questioned the value of a college education, especially given its high cost and the uncertain job market. From 2022 to 2024, tech companies, having over hired during the pandemic, began laying off white-collar workers in large numbers. Advancements in AI and automation started to replace roles that were once entry-level, as these technologies enhanced company productivity and reduced costs.

Previously, staff were seen as valuable resources; now, they are often viewed as expenses. The respect once accorded to highly skilled talent seems to be a relic of the past. This shift has been particularly challenging for recent college graduates seeking employment. AI has not only elevated the standard of average performance but also begun to supplant junior roles, which were more prone to errors and slower output compared to senior positions. With a surge of layoffs in big tech companies, experienced professionals are now competing for the same roles as entry-level candidates, further intensifying job market competition.

Because of the current market, we need to change our mindset from getting a job to getting a career. In this context, understanding the difference between a job and a career becomes crucial. A job is a specific position of employment, while a career is a pursuit in a field or profession, often requiring specialized training and offering lifelong progression. The stability once associated with white-collar jobs, especially for top academic performers, is no longer guaranteed. With an oversupply of job seekers and ongoing layoffs, finding traditional employment has become more challenging. In this new era, forging one's career path is more vital than ever. While a job may not provide long-term security, a career, built on individual strengths and adaptability, can offer enduring opportunities.

Damon Hernandez (CEO of Mixx Reality) and Ferhan Özkan (Co-Founder of XR Bootcamp) highlight the importance for designers and creators to distinguish themselves by capitalizing on their unique strengths and skills, particularly in response to the demands of the market. For example, in the spatial design app, the key to innovation often lies in blending diverse interests or hobbies with game design. Integrating elements from fields like cooking, music, architecture, film, or acting can lead to groundbreaking developments and creative breakthroughs. The best innovative games or apps normally blend a specific field of knowledge of expertise in the spatial design field. Another effective strategy is collaboration with subject matter experts to tackle specific challenges. A prime example of this is Virtuleap, where XR developers have partnered with neuroscientists to develop a game aimed at enhancing brain function. This collaboration demonstrates the significant impact and potential of combining expertise from different domains.

Antony Vitillo (CTO at VRROOM), highlighted the versatility in career paths within the field of spatial design. Whether working for companies, freelancing, pursuing art, design, blogging, or starting a business, the options are diverse. However, he emphasized the importance of practical experience, urging individuals to dive into projects and get their hands "dirty." Antony also pointed out that spatial design, being a blend of technology and multimedia, benefits from collaborative efforts across multiple disciplines. He encourages joining events and communities to work collaboratively rather than in isolation. Frank Shi (Co-Founder of Paper Triangles), acknowledging Gen Z's inherent comfort with the internet and digital tools, sees this as an advantage for innovation and financial success. He underscores the necessity of dedication and consistent effort, noting that achieving success typically requires years of committed work. While recognizing the plethora of free resources available to Gen Z, Frank stresses the importance of their commitment and hard work to leverage these opportunities effectively.

Evaluating Long-Term XR Investments

If you want to start your own company, here's the advice from an investor's point of view. Amy LaMeyer (WXR Fund) outlined her approach for evaluating long-term XR investments, focusing on the problem being solved, market size, the startup's dependence on hardware, and the founders' passion. They also discussed the impact of global events on the XR industry, noting reduced ability to sell, longer sales cycles, slower growth, and difficulties in raising money but also an increase in available talent.

When she evaluates the long-term potential of immersive technology investments, it's crucial to consider several key factors. Firstly, the extent of a startup's dependence on hardware is a significant aspect, as it can influence scalability and market adaptability. Understanding market expectations, including the size and growth potential, is vital for assessing the likely demand and commercial viability. The core of the evaluation centers around whether the solution effectively solves a real-world problem, which is often a strong indicator of its potential success. Additionally, the passion and determination of the founders play an important role in driving the startup's resilience and adaptability.

How to Break into the Industry

Thomas Van Bouwel has illuminated pathways for engaging Gen Z in software development, underscoring the significance of immersive, hands-on education via game jams and hackathons. He notes that while no-code and low-code platforms serve as excellent introductory tools, the swift expansion of the spatial design sector might surpass these platforms' capacities to assimilate emerging features. Thus, Thomas underscores the indispensable value of coding proficiency for crafting tailor-made digital experiences.

Lee Vermeulen stresses the importance of starting game development with simpler, non-extended reality (non-XR) games, such as 2D or 3D, before diving into VR game design. This approach, he argues, lays a more solid foundation than beginning directly with VR. Lee points out the intricate challenges of crafting a high-quality VR experience and cautions that subpar VR games might deter users, particularly due to issues like motion sickness and the unrefined nature of many VR games. He advises beginning with traditional game development methods to achieve high-quality results, which can then be transitioned into VR projects. Moreover, Lee encourages emerging spatial designers to engage in hands-on learning experiences like hackathons, focusing on creating simple yet well-executed games to refine their skills.

Sam Hessenauer, highlighting a drive for innovation, urges young people to master the use of advanced language models and prototyping tools to enhance their work. By acquiring essential programming skills and utilizing tools like ChatGPT, project development can be significantly improved. Sam, with his experience in Unity and advanced spatial computing devices like the Quest 3, envisions a future rich with multimodal, ubiquitous AR, integrating AI and spatial tracking into everyday eyewear. This vision, he believes, will radically alter daily life. His team is at the forefront of merging spatial computing with on-device AI in mixed-reality environments, paving the way for these technologies to become universally adopted tools in the future.

Rahel Demant, Co-Founder of XR Bootcamp, emphasizes the importance of cultivating creativity, continuous skill acquisition, and staying updated with industry trends. Parallel to this, Ferhan Özkan, also a Co-Founder of XR Bootcamp, highlights the necessity of a development approach centered on rapid prototyping, ongoing iteration, and comprehensive testing.

Echoing these sentiments, Dirk Schmidt and Jason Shuster from BizzTech advocate for the integration of AI in career development within the metaverse. They recommend mastering AI as a job enhancement tool, noting that while AI won't completely replace design work, it will greatly increase efficiency and streamline operations. They suggest a collaborative model where professionals allow AI to perform about 80% of a task, stepping in with their unique expertise to complete the final 20%.

Stay Connected

Alan Smithson, Co-Founder of METAVRSE, suggested joining organizations such as the VR/AR Association,[85] XR Women,[86] and more to learn and contribute. He emphasized the importance of community in fostering motivation and creating a sense of purpose, particularly in the development of new technologies.

AI Replacing Human Jobs versus Integration

In the rapidly evolving landscape of technology, AI-driven devices like ChatGPT, Rabbit OS, and various generative AI tools are emerging frequently. These advancements lead

---

[85] https://www.thevrara.com
[86] https://www.xrwomen.com

to a shift where machines perform more tasks, increasingly automating processes. The interaction with AI has progressed from merely seeking answers to instructing AI to execute specific tasks, and now, AI can accomplish many assigned tasks autonomously. This shift has significant implications across industries: from a business perspective, it accelerates production and reduces costs. However, for the workforce, this technological surge makes securing traditional jobs more challenging than before.

AI Took Our Jobs

In 2024, a survey revealed that about a quarter of global CEOs anticipate cutting over 5% of their staff as generative AI technology becomes more prevalent. This trend is most likely to affect the media, entertainment, banking, insurance, and logistics sectors, where AI is expected to handle tasks traditionally performed by white-collar workers. However, industries like engineering, construction, and technology may experience less impact. The adoption of AI is seen to increase productivity by automating routine tasks. Despite job cut concerns, UK businesses are optimistic about AI leading to headcount increases, correlating with the growth and adoption of generative AI.[87]

If you're trading your time for money through your expertise, you may find AI as a competitor. But if you're in product creation, AI can be a significant ally, streamlining your workflow. Take graphic designers, for example: AI can accelerate their creative process by generating initial design concepts from typed descriptions. However, this also allows clients to bypass designers entirely, using AI tools like DALL-E or Midjourney for logo creation. Professional logo design, typically priced between $250 and $5000+, is now challenged by these cost-effective AI solutions. Clients might only need part-time remote designers for tweaks, making AI-generated logos a go-to for startups on tight budgets. Companies with higher budgets would likely opt for traditional, higher cost customized design services.

---

[87] Brian-Damien Morgan, Readwrite, https://readwrite.com/pwc-annual-global-report-predicts-jobs-cuts-ahead-in-2024, accessed Jan. 2024.

David Colleen offers a perspective on AI and job displacement. He pointed out that during COVID-19, there was a high demand for in-person assistants in hotels, hospitals, and trade shows – roles that were difficult to fill. Digital humans help bridge this gap, providing services in areas where there is little interest in traditional employment. Moreover, today's younger generation benefits from more accessible tools and affordable devices, a stark contrast to earlier times. Echoing Albert Einstein's words, "The true sign of intelligence is not knowledge but imagination," Colleen suggests that the focus should shift from production to ideation.

In this scenario, it's advantageous to shift our mindset towards becoming a product owner and creating a business that leverages AI benefits. Rather than seeking specific jobs that lack direct human interaction, it's crucial to remain adaptable and open to learning new skills and technologies as they emerge. This approach not only aligns with the evolving job market but also positions you to capitalize on AI advancements.

AI Integration

Lorelle VanFossen shared her optimistic view that AI would help people discover their passions and replace certain jobs, allowing experts to thrive, and everyone to start pursuing their passion projects/work. Charlie Fink pointed out that even though AI tools simplify the creative process by eliminating much of the manual labor, we haven't seen significantly unique, high-quality intellectual projects come out of it yet. So even though the labor is being reduced, the highly innovative IP is still hard to produce.

Therefore, in the age of AI, the pursuit of higher-level creativity and the development of unique intellectual properties are the most important things to do.

Gigi Johnson envisions a future where creating immersive environments becomes seamless and accessible even to those without specialized skills. She foresees this democratization of technology facilitating faster production and a diverse range of outputs. For instance, a 22-year-old innovator can utilize AI tools to develop products, encountering minimal barriers. Gigi emphasizes that crafting unique intellectual properties (IP) and producing outstanding products is the new challenge.

She underscores the critical role of AI in customizing content for varied audiences and overcoming language barriers. Gigi views AI as a leveling force in business, reducing the traditional edge held by larger corporations. She likens this progression to a "Canva for VR," enabling users to effortlessly create content using templates.

Further, Gigi expanded on AI's increasing influence in the music and gaming industries. She emphasized its transformative role in developing virtual environments, interactive backgrounds, and its capability for character substitution in videos. Intellectual property rights were a significant topic, with Gigi emphasizing the need to track the origin of assets employed in AI models. Her insights highlighted the vast potential of AI tools and the importance of both embracing their evolution and integrating them thoughtfully.

Charlie Fink discusses the potential impact of AI on content creation and filmmaking. He highlights that AI can enhance various aspects of movie production, such as costume design, lighting design, and location shooting logistics. He mentions the launch of OpenAI's app store and predicts that it will offer tools for filmmakers and social media professionals. He believes that these tools will influence the type of content produced and increase production speed.

Additionally, Charlie suggests that while AI may make certain tasks easier, it will not replace essential roles like set designers or costume designers. However, he acknowledges that AI has remarkable potential but emphasizes the need to fully understand its capabilities before diving too deeply into implementation. He mentioned that AI stands as a transformative force in streamlining 3D content creation. While AI significantly assists in design, it remains under human oversight. The process begins with AI, but it's the designers who refine and enhance the outcomes, evident in AI's swift integration into platforms like Adobe.

Alan Smithson believes AI can enhance spatial design by offering user-specific content and employing generative AI for personalized experiences. He sees AI's potential in transforming 2D art into 3D and creating lifelike 3D objects from text descriptions. Additionally, conversational AI could enable interactions with non-player characters in digital environments. Alan also discusses the risks and ethical considerations of AI in his blog *AI vs Humans*,[88] delving into the complex relationship between AI advancements and human roles.

Jason Marsh emphasizes the critical role of AI and Spatial Data Visualization in managing and understanding risks, especially in complex project management scenarios. He also noted the utility of spatial design in representing data. This approach is particularly valuable in environmental risk assessments and supply chain management, offering a clearer visualization of intricate data sets.

Technology Convergence in Industries

Robin Moulder has highlighted the revolutionary role of AI in enhancing personalized training simulations across various sectors, including healthcare, aviation, and manufacturing. They particularly emphasized AI's ability to enable natural and intuitive user interactions, using hand signals as a key example of its potential. Looking ahead, Robin envisions a future where context-sensitive information is dynamically produced and conveyed through AR and MR. In the domains of gaming and entertainment, they pointed out AI's prowess in directing characters, molding lifelike behaviors, and creating rich, dynamic narratives. By focusing on AI's role in training simulations, Robin underscored its capability to produce evolving content, thus deepening the learning experience with enhanced immersion and realism.

Julie Smithson also stresses the significance of immersive technology in advancing training across critical sectors. This shift in technology, evident through cost reductions and accelerated learning processes, is reshaping skills development. For example, her

---

[88] AI vs Humans, https://aivshumans.ai, accessed Jan. 2024

partnership with Siemens Healthineers has transformed education in healthcare by granting virtual access to high-value medical equipment, enabling in-depth learning without the need for physical presence. In the retail sector, there is a notable evolution in redefining customer experiences, particularly in facing challenges like product availability. Furthermore, contemporary business practices are increasingly focusing on deep collaboration, moving from traditional transaction-based approaches to more cohesive partnerships. This trend, particularly using spatial design technologies, mirrors the innovative trajectories in today's interconnected, tech-centric business environment.

To Code or Not to Code?

Does a designer need to learn to code? With the widespread application of AI, the choice between mastering coding and opting for no-code solutions has become a pivotal topic. AI advancements have streamlined software development significantly, allowing users to create products effortlessly using text or voice commands. This rapid development, propelled further by Brain-Computer Interface (BCI) devices, leads to what Terry Schussler envisions as the era of "disposable" software, where software creation is almost effortless. Yet, for those seeking to develop unique intellectual property, coding skills remain crucial. While no-code tools may label users as consumers, coding enables one to be a creator and potentially profit from their innovation.

Marc Mathys, CEO of CNS Therapy, notes that the choice between coding and no coding boils down to a bottom-up versus top-down approach in product creation. The quality of the product is paramount, regardless of the approach taken.

Diverse tech leaders express varying opinions on this matter. Proponents of no-code, like Matt Wood of AWS and Chris Wanstrath, former CEO of GitHub, foresee a future where coding becomes obsolete, replaced by intuitive natural language interfaces. On the other hand, advocates for coding, such as Bill Gates and Tim Cook, emphasize its importance in fostering critical thinking and addressing global challenges.

From a bottom-up perspective, coding is essential for understanding technology infrastructure and creating innovative, customizable solutions. This approach, while demanding, balances creativity with practicality. For instance, developers using tools like Unity can push technological boundaries. Thomas Van Bouwel (VR Developer on Cubism & Laser Dance) emphasizes the fundamental understanding that coding offers. Coding knowledge is vital, even when working with no-code tools, as it facilitates adapting to the fast-evolving landscape of spatial computing tools and allows for customization and keeping pace with new developments. Jeremy Kress, a software engineer, notes that whether it's a code or no-code platform, both necessitate developers for their creation and maintenance. Code platforms typically precede, forming the basis upon which no-code platforms are developed. These no-code platforms still rely on developers for their construction, ongoing maintenance, and updates.

Conversely, the top-down approach with no-code tools allows for quick product visualization and collaboration. Tools like ShapesXR enable efficient idea development and cross-disciplinary communication. Predictions by experts like Gigi Johnson suggest that in the future, creating immersive environments will become accessible to all, leading to faster production and varied outputs. AI's role in content customization for individual audiences is also highlighted.

Ultimately, the decision to learn coding depends on individual goals. Coding offers flexibility for building platforms and innovating features, while no-code tools are ideal for rapid prototyping and design-focused tasks. The choice should align with one's objectives and strengths. Alex Fernandez (Co-Founder at Nspire) underscores the importance of skill diversification. For those not inclined towards programming, excelling in areas like ideation, experience design, animation, storytelling, or business acumen is crucial. Excelling in at least one domain is key to distinguishing oneself in the field of development, where basic qualifications often overlap.

Conclusion

Considering the shifts brought on by AI, economic downturns, and layoffs, it's imperative that we reposition ourselves, embracing the cycle of learning, unlearning, and relearning to adapt to this new era. Drawing from the wisdom of 38 industry leaders, the consensus is clear: pursue your passions with unwavering determination, and proactively showcase your accomplishments on platforms like LinkedIn to enhance your professional visibility. Support the successes of others, gravitate towards growth opportunities in emerging industries that align with your strengths, and prioritize roles that necessitate human interaction—such as those in healthcare and education—to mitigate the risk of automation. Bolster your online presence by acquiring coding skills and generating your own intellectual property. When initiating contact on LinkedIn, lead with offering value prior to seeking assistance. Engage in public speaking or organize events to solidify your professional reputation, embrace challenges that are greater than oneself to promote collaboration, and in saturated markets, differentiate yourself by merging your interests and expertise to address genuine needs.

This book aims to equip you for success in the era of spatial design. Should you have any inquiries or require assistance, please don't hesitate to connect with me on LinkedIn @dominiquewu, and consider joining the XReality Pro LinkedIn @xrealitypro. To get a response to your post on LinkedIn, simply tag me or XRealityPro, and your queries will be addressed. Thank you for engaging with this book. I look forward to connecting with you soon.

Glossary

A-Frame: An open-source web framework for building virtual reality (VR) experiences. It is primarily used for building VR applications that run on web browsers.

AGI (Artificial General Intelligence): A level of artificial intelligence where a machine can understand, learn, and apply its intelligence broadly and flexibly, like a human's cognitive abilities.

AI (Artificial Intelligence): A branch of computer science focusing on creating intelligent machines or software capable of tasks that typically require human intelligence, such as understanding speech, visual perception, and decision-making.

AI Digital Assistant: A technology that assists users through voice or gesture commands, often equipped with advanced features like iris scanning for a personalized experience.

Android and iOS Devices: Platforms that support a variety of AR/VR applications and experiences, with a wide user base and accessible development tools.

Apple Vision Pro: A headset using visionOS for immersive experiences with features like eye tracking, hand gestures, voice commands, and a digital crown for immersion control.

AR (Augmented Reality): A technology that overlays digital information onto the real-world environment, enhancing the user's perception of reality.

ARKit: A framework by Apple for developing augmented reality (AR) apps for iOS devices. It allows developers to use iPhone and iPad hardware to create immersive AR experiences.

Augmented World Expo (AWE): An annual conference and expo focused on AR and VR technologies. It brings together a mix of industry professionals, technology pioneers, and enthusiasts to discuss advancements in the AR/VR industry.

Avatar Personalization: Allowing users to customize their avatars, reflecting their personal style and identity in virtual environments.

Blender Software: An open-source 3D computer graphics software used for creating animated films, visual effects, art, 3D printed models, motion graphics, interactive 3D applications, virtual reality, and computer games.

ChatGPT: An AI language model developed by OpenAI, designed to generate human-like text based on the input it receives. It's used for a variety of applications, including conversation simulation, text completion, and information queries.

Cognitive Load Reduction: Simplifying user interfaces and interactions to reduce cognitive strain, making technology more accessible and user-friendly.

DALL-E: An AI program created by OpenAI that generates images from textual descriptions, using a variant of the GPT-3 algorithm. It's known for its ability to create imaginative and diverse images based on descriptive language.

Data Self-Sovereignty: Ensuring transparency and user consent in data collection and usage in spatial design applications.

Digital Twin: Virtual representation of physical objects or systems used for various purposes, including simulation, analysis, and control.

Diverse Representation: Representing a wide range of cultures, identities, and abilities in avatars, environments, and narratives within XR spaces.

Dyslexie Font: A typeface designed to improve readability for individuals with dyslexia, especially effective in VR environments.

Environmental Mapping: The process of creating a digital map of a surrounding area, allowing devices to understand the layout and dimensions of a space.

Error Reduction Strategies: Techniques such as providing "Undo" options, tutorials, and visual, auditory, and haptic feedback to minimize errors in user interactions.

Field of View (FOV): The extent of the observable world that can be seen at any given moment. In the context of VR/AR, it refers to the range of the visual field covered by the display.

Figma: A cloud-based design tool used for interface design, primarily for web and mobile app layouts. It enables designers to collaborate in real-time, making it a popular tool for UX/UI design projects.

Flow State: A state of deep engagement and focus in an activity, often used as a benchmark for immersive experiences.

Gamification: The application of game-design elements and game principles in non-game contexts. It is used to improve user engagement, organizational productivity, learning, and other activities.

GIS (Geographic Information Systems): Systems for capturing, storing, checking, and displaying data related to positions on Earth's surface.

GPS (Global Positioning System): A satellite-based navigation system that provides location and time information anywhere on or near the Earth where there is an unobstructed line of sight to four or more GPS satellites.

Guardian System: Defined play areas and virtual boundaries for safety in VR environments.

Haptic Feedback: A technology that simulates the sense of touch by applying forces, vibrations, or motions to the user.

Head-Mounted Displays (HMDs): A type of wearable technology that displays images and data directly in front of the user's eyes. HMDs are commonly used in virtual reality (VR) and augmented reality (AR) systems.

Hololens 2: Microsoft's mixed reality head-mounted display used in various sectors for enhanced accuracy and productivity.

HTC Vive XR Elite: A lightweight, convertible headset for mixed reality with high-resolution passthrough, detachable batteries, and skeletal-level hand tracking.

Immersive Design: Creating realistic environments and interactions to enhance the user's sense of presence.

Interactivity in Spatial Design: Enhancing user engagement through interactive elements and immersive experiences in virtual environments.

Interpupillary Distance (IPD): The distance between the centers of the pupils of the eyes. Accurately measuring IPD is important for the proper alignment of lenses in devices like binoculars, VR headsets, etc.

IoT (Internet of Things): A network of physical objects embedded with sensors, software, and other technologies for connecting and exchanging data with other devices and systems over the Internet.

Locomotion: Incorporating various movement methods like arm swinging, real walking, vehicle-based movement, or teleportation for diverse and comfortable navigation in VR.

Magic Leap 2: An AR device for enterprise use with a wide field of view, Dynamic Dimming technology, and various input methods including hand and eye-tracking.

Metaverse: A collective virtual shared space, created by the convergence of virtually enhanced physical reality, augmented reality, and the internet. It's often described as a hypothetical iteration of the Internet, supporting persistent online 3D virtual environments.

Meta Quest 3: A mixed reality headset with 4K resolution, Snapdragon XR2 Gen 2 processor, and advanced sensors for immersive interactions.

Microsoft Inclusive Design: Principles and practices aimed at creating accessible technology for a wide range of users.

Mirror Virtual Environment (MVE): A design approach where virtual environments closely align with physical world orientation and interaction patterns.

MR (Mixed Reality): A blend of real and virtual worlds to produce new environments where physical and digital objects co-exist and interact in real time.

MRTK (Mixed Reality Toolkit): A collection of scripts and components intended to accelerate the development of mixed reality applications, particularly those targeting Microsoft HoloLens and Windows Mixed Reality headsets.

Natural User Interface (NUI): Interfaces that enable interaction between humans and machines using natural human actions, like voice commands, eye movements, or hand gestures.

No-Code: A software development approach that allows non-programmers to create software applications using graphical user interfaces and configuration instead of traditional computer programming. It enables quicker development and deployment of applications.

Onboarding: Guiding users through spatial design environments with tutorials and onboarding processes to ensure understanding and effective use.

Open AR Cloud Association (OARC): Promoting open standards and secure environments for the Metaverse.

Passthrough: A feature in VR/AR devices that allows users to see the real world through cameras embedded in the device, often used for safety and awareness.

Persona Spectrum: A concept from the Microsoft Inclusive Toolkit highlighting that designing for permanent disabilities also benefits those with temporary or situational limitations.

Photogrammetry: The science of making measurements from photographs, often used for mapping and 3D modeling.

Pico 4: A VR headset by ByteDance with pancake lenses, LCD displays, real-time hand tracking, and passthrough mode.

Prototype Tools: Software and applications like ShapesXR and Horizon Worlds that facilitate rapid development and testing in spatial design.

Quest 3: A mixed reality device known for room scanning and understanding spatial layouts, representing a transition to spatial computing.

Rapid Prototyping: Quickly transforming concepts into tangible prototypes to test and refine innovative projects.

Robot-Sighted Guides: Technologies developed to assist people with low vision in navigating and avoiding obstacles in XR environments.

Self-Sovereign Identity (SSI): Empowering users with control over their personal information in the digital realm.

Skeuomorphism: Utilizing familiar real-world cues in virtual environments to enhance user experience, making these environments intuitive and immersive.

SLAM (Simultaneous Localization and Mapping): A process used in robotics and AR/VR technologies to map an environment while simultaneously keeping track of the location within it.

Software Development Kit (SDK): A set of software tools and programs used by developers to create applications for specific platforms or frameworks. SDKs typically include APIs, programming tools, and documentation.

SPAI (Spatial Artificial Intelligence): A term proposed to reflect the fusion of XR and AI, where AI enhances XR technologies for more natural interactions and understanding of spatial relationships.

SparkAR: A platform and toolkit from Facebook for building augmented reality experiences for mobile devices. It allows creators to develop AR effects for Facebook and Instagram.

Spatial Audio Guides: Audio tools used in XR to enhance navigation and interaction, are particularly beneficial for users with visual impairments.

Spatial Computing: A broad concept involving the integration of digital information with our physical environment. It uses technologies like AI, VR, AR, GPS, IoT, and robotics to enhance real-world interactions.

Spatial Design: A human-centered, immersive experience design that integrates UX, 3D technologies, and AI. It focuses on creating meaningful connections in various environments.

Starlink: A satellite internet constellation being constructed by SpaceX to provide satellite Internet access. The constellation will consist of thousands of mass-produced small satellites in low Earth orbit, working in combination with ground transceivers.

SwiftUI: A user interface toolkit that lets iOS app developers design views with a declarative Swift syntax. It's used to build user interfaces across all Apple platforms with Swift code.

Tunnel Vision: A visual impairment where peripheral vision is reduced, causing a decrease in the visual field. It can be a literal medical condition or metaphorically describe a focus on a single aspect of a problem, ignoring broader considerations.

User Experience (UX) Design: Involves designing products with a focus on the end-user's interaction, blending design theory with research, user testing, and development processes.

Varjo: Specializes in high-end virtual and mixed reality headsets for professional use.

Virtual Training Simulations: Simulated environments for training purposes, where tasks mimic real-life scenarios for effective skill development.

Visual Comfort: Implementing gentle lighting, soothing color schemes, simple textures, and clear depth cues to reduce eye strain and discomfort in virtual environments.

VR (Virtual Reality): A fully immersive digital environment that replaces the user's real-world environment, often through a head-mounted display.

Xcode: An integrated development environment (IDE) for macOS, used for developing software for macOS, iOS, iPadOS, watchOS, and tvOS.

WebXR: A standard for accessing VR and AR devices, including sensors and head-mounted displays, on the web. It enables the creation of immersive web experiences that can be accessed through a browser.

X Reality Safety Intelligence (XRSI): Focusing on safety, privacy, and ethical considerations in emerging technologies.

XR (Extended Reality): A collective term for immersive technologies, including Augmented Reality (AR), Virtual Reality (VR), and Mixed Reality (MR). It represents the integration of digital and physical realities.

XR (Extended Reality) Design: Encompasses design, interaction, and 3D skills, focusing on immersive storytelling in virtual and mixed realities.

XR Access: A community focused on making virtual, augmented, and mixed reality accessible to people with disabilities.

XR Guild: Advocating for ethical practices and responsible innovation in XR and AI technologies.

XREAL Air 2: AR glasses noted for their design, Micro-LED displays, wide field of view, and compatibility with various devices.

About the Author

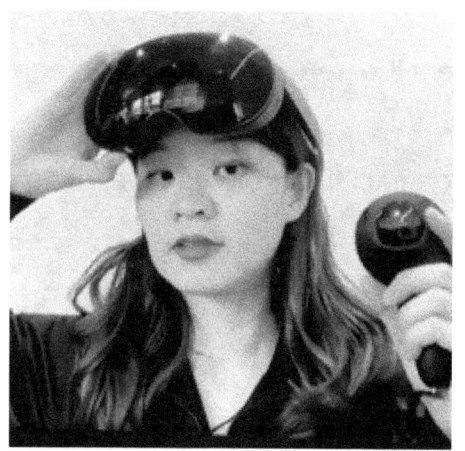

Dominique Wu is known for her dedication to creating user-centric spatial interfaces and conducting detailed user research and testing within 3D environments. Her expertise has allowed her to provide valuable consultancy services to notable companies, including Meta and Walmart's Store 8 innovation hub. Beyond her consultancy role, Dominique is at the helm of Hummingbirdsday Design Studio and XReality Pro, where she crafts spatial design solutions tailored to a wide range of industries. Her passion for the field drives her to share her insights and encourage exploration of spatial design, both in professional forums such as AWE and academic circles.

As an Adjunct Professor at Cañada College, Dominique is equally committed to XR and Spatial Computing education. She has utilized her UX design skills to make contributions to the immersive technology sector over the past decade, impacting leading companies and the industry at large.

Dominique also plays a pivotal role in building a vibrant XR community, having engaged over 20,000 individuals in the USA through tutorials, speaking engagements, and hackathons associated with XReality Pro. She facilitates weekly virtual meetings that bring together spatial design experts, fostering a space for learning and networking. Dominique's projects, particularly those involving the development of spatial design prototypes using Unity and the crafting of user-friendly spatial interfaces, are focused on improving user experiences through innovative and practical design solutions.

Praise For Author

At this pivotal moment in time, as the shift from two dimensional to spatial computing becomes increasingly relevant, Dominque Wu has provided an in-depth guide to supply creators with the knowledge to leap into the 3D space. For the majority of people to adopt a new computing paradigm (including new digital devices), three pillars must align: cost/affordability, comfort and content/interest. Dominique's focus on design in this book specifically addresses two of the three pillars by providing detailed methods to enable usability and the creation of interesting, entertaining and/or productivity enhancing content. I highly recommend this book, especially for creators that are looking to quickly understand the shift from 2D to spatial and the vast opportunities of this new wave of computing. - Amy LaMeyer, Managing Partner of the WXR Fund

Dominique has since early days been a visionary and passionate leader in the XR community, rallying the industry. - Ben Erwin, Creator of The Poly Awards

Dominique has brought together many experts who are paving the road for the future of computing. I highly recommend this book which is packed full of valuable industry knowledge. - Alex Fernandez, Co-Founder of Nspire Create Labs

Breaking the 2D Paradigm: XR Spatial Design is a must-read for anyone interested in the future of design. Author Dominique Wu, a leading expert in XR (extended reality) design, takes readers on a journey through the emerging world of spatial computing, where the boundaries between the physical and digital are dissolving. Wu argues that traditional 2D design paradigms are no longer sufficient for the immersive and interactive experiences that XR technologies make possible. She introduces readers to the core concepts of XR design, such as presence, embodiment, and spatial thinking, and provides practical guidance on how to create XR experiences that are both functional and engaging.

Here are some of the things I liked most about the book: It is well-written and easy to understand, even for those who are new to XR. Wu avoids using technical jargon and explains complex concepts in a clear and concise way. It is packed with practical advice and case studies. Wu draws on her own experience as an XR designer to provide readers with real-world examples of how to apply the principles she discusses.

It is inspiring and thought-provoking. Wu challenges readers to think about the potential of XR to transform the way we live, work, and play. If you are a designer, developer, entrepreneur, or anyone who is interested in the future of technology, I highly recommend reading Breaking the 2D Paradigm: XR Spatial Design. It is a valuable resource that will help you to prepare for the coming wave of XR innovation. In addition to the above, here are some specific quotes from the book that I found to be particularly insightful:

"XR is not just about creating new technologies; it is about creating new ways of being in the world."

"The most important thing about XR design is to focus on the human experience."

"XR has the potential to revolutionize every aspect of our lives, from the way we work and learn to the way we shop and entertain ourselves."

- Marc Mathys, CEO at CNS Therapy

More than just a book on VR/AR/XR, "Spatial Design: Breaking the 2D Paradigm" discusses current trends and touches upon the influence of Artificial Intelligence on tomorrow's spatial design concepts. A must-read for anyone passionate about the intersection of technology and creativity. - J. Teutloff, President, JV-Global LLC

This book provides a timely and essential framework for understanding the design principles shaping the future of human-computer interaction. A must-read for anyone involved in creating immersive experiences. This book goes beyond technical trends to explore the enduring design concepts that will pave the way for successful XR projects. With my decades of experience in building real-time systems, I believe the book's perspective on the importance of foundational design in a rapidly evolving technological landscape is invaluable. The emphasis on 'timeless patterns' underscores the need for resilient design strategies in the face of ever-changing XR technologies. I appreciate the book's holistic approach to spatial design, integrating the needs of the human user on every level – psychological, physical, and social. The transition from 2D to 3D design concepts is explored with clarity, giving designers the tools to adapt to this exciting paradigm shift. - Chris McNally, Co-Founder of iMcNally